Theology and Globalisation:
A Commentary

by Rowan Gill

ATF Press
Adelaide

Theology and Globalistion:

A Commentary

by Rowan Gill

ATF Press
Adelaide

First published 2005

ISBN 1 920691 49 9

Published by
ATF Press
An imprint of the Australian Theological Forum
P O Box 504
Hindmarsh
SA 5007
ABN 68 314 074 034
www.atfpress.com

Cover design by Openbook Print, Adelaide, Australia
Printed by Kanisius Press, Yogyakarta - Indonesia
www.kanisiusmedia.com

To

my wife Sylvia

and to my son

Greg

Contents

Contents

Introduction

This book is a theological reflection and commentary on the contemporary phenomenon of globalisation.

The first chapter is an introduction to the topic in which I examine the thought of the leading American ethicist Max Stackhouse and his approach to the topic of globalisation. I find his work problematic from a number of perspectives.

The second chapter is an exposition of Augustinian political theory as it comes to bear upon the topic of globalisation. This will be important in the final part of this book.

The third chapter is a sketch of the relationship between the 'people of God' and 'empires' throughout the last three thousand years. This gives a longitudinal approach to the topic.

The phenomenon of globalisation is analysed in the fourth chapter. First, by Thomas L Friedman and then by Joseph Stiglitz. They give an insiders view of globalisation and is followed by a critique of their views by Cynthia Moe-Lobeda, Lesslie Newbigin, Davis McCaughey and myself.

In the fifth chapter of the book I examine 'imperial America' and argue that globalisation is an outcropping of America as an 'imperial power'. I examine this feature of American life in its original geographical expansion, the use of the term 'manifest destiny' in its political rhetoric and the present situation in which America is the only super power in the world.

The final chapter holds that forces of convergence in the world of the twentieth century move toward world government. I argue that there needs to be an ethical basis drawn from the world's religions as a foundation for such a government. Further, there needs to be a strong emphasis upon justice in such a world. I do not spell out how such a world government is to be brought into being but something like it, I suggest, will have to come about.

The age of chivalry is gone. That of sophisters, economists and calculators has succeeded and the glory of Europe is extinguished forever.
(Edmund Burke, eighteenth century)

The trial by market everything must come to.
(Robert Frost 1916)

Max Stackhouse and Globalisation

Of all Christian theologians, Max L Stackhouse, Professor of Christian Ethics at Princeton Theological Seminary, has been at the forefront of American theologians advocating a Christian approach to globalisation.[1]

In examining a recent article of October 2003, Stackhouse's writing is expansive, buoyant and all-encompassing as he describes management in politics, the ecology, the markets, civil society, and the corporations, in what is essentially a putting forth of a worldview.[2] Of note is that there is no mention of the United Nations. The distinct impression one is left with is of global movements that are expanding and enabling humanity's capacities for growth, well-being and the sense of justice. However, he has to admit toward the end that there is a snake in paradise—witness the Enron and Arthur Andersen and World Com collapses in the United States—the picture is not completely rosy and—in a more sombre mood—something must be done. Stackhouse, again soberly, recalls community leadership, stewardship and a sense of vocation—rich words in the American Protestant religious and business lexicons—and concludes by saying that Protestantism—as if it were only a series of Protestant problems he is describing(!)—should look to its roots.[3]

I would describe Stackhouse's personal approach to the whole matter as bipolar,[4] that is, an expansiveness combined with a despair, and I wonder about his approach to capitalism. Indeed, I am concerned that in this article, whether in a long

---

1. This has been evident at least since Max L Stackhouse, *Apologia: Contextualization, Globalization, and Mission in Theological Education* (Grand Rapids: Eerdman, 1988).
2. Max L Stackhouse, 'Spheres of Management: Social, Ethical and Theological Reflections', *Theology Today* 60 (October 2003): 370-383.
3. He seems to think that mainline churches in the US are too preoccupied with combative matters with lesser issues such as homosexuality than to be involved in the reconstruction of the globe (381).
4. I am aware that this is also a psychiatric term.

academic life of supporting and expounding capitalism, he might have espied a capitalism or had a personal view of capitalism which has not after all progressed beyond Weber's 'iron cage'.[5] That is, capitalism—even in a global context —might be like a stuck gramophone needle, might be creating its own demons, might be curved in upon itself and therefore producing problems which are a function of itself with no prospect of real further progress beyond its own given.

Stackhouse's essay seems ultimately weary. It can only propound the tired clichés of the past for a new situation that has arisen for global capitalism and the international Christian church, that is after September 11 2001, even if Stackhouse is only really interested in Protestantism.

In another essay by Stackhouse, a long 1995 essay 'Christian Social Ethics in a Global Era: Reforming Protestant Views',[6] was written in the new situation brought about by the fall of the Berlin Wall and the collapse of Communism in Eastern Europe. In this event it was apparent to many what were the true issues regarding church, economics, among other things, as they impacted upon the then current stances that had not been foreseen until then (see the Preface, 7). Stackhouse was not free from making errors regarding the foreseeable future in 1995!:

> At another level, we are now seeing the most massive 'builddown' of military forces and weaponry ever, as state after state demobilizes soldiers, machinery, nuclear weaponry and military industries, from Moscow to Washington . . . (18).[7]

The clue to this post-Berlin wall dynamic is found in the following:

---

5.   Max Weber, *The Protestant Ethic and the Spirit of Capitalism* (1904–5).
6.   In *Christian Social Ethics in a Global Era*, Abingdon Press Studies in Christian Ethics and Economic Life xxi, (Nashville: Abingdon Press, 1995), 11–93. All page references are included in the body of our text.
7.   The irony of this is borne out by Joseph Stiglitz, *Globalization and its Discontents* (Camberwell, Vic: Allen Lane, 2002), 176-177.

> It is . . . likely that the Reformed theological
> tradition has it right: humans were distinguished
> from the beasts when they knelt down and saw
> *themselves* as tools of a loving and just God, called
> to be stewards of the earth where it manifested
> God's designs and to redesign the world where it
> was fallen.[8]

This is a crude, instrumentalist doctrine of election, and, however softened by talk of a loving God, serves as the motivation of the essay in its privileging of Protestantism, capitalism, and globalisation. It is not like an Islamic *monotheism* because there is a mention of the Trinity (if rather desultorily) (45), and two mentions of Christology (42, 68); but neither trinitarian nor christological thought is woven into the main thrust of the essay's argument. Nor is a doctrine of salvation or atonement propounded, but only the inner holiness of the process (19, 23, 24, 25, 30, 37, 45, 52).

From this centre capitalism, corporations and globalisation are rightly formed as a great challenge to the Protestant churches, and the task is to subdue and rule the earth.

Along the way many things are discarded: Catholic approaches and virtue ethics (65–6), socialism (*passim*), the 'underside' of the community (66), nature (49–54); he has an ambivalent view of hierarchy (59–63).

Stackhouse strictly adheres to absolutes (64–5). He writes:

> My central hypothesis is that in the faithful
> Protestant churches the ultimate questions are
> posed; thus the great dualism that can control
> and challenge hierarchy where it is evil, and
> preserve it where it supports life, is made vital in
> people's minds and hearts (56).

Stackhouse believes all this is supra-governmental. He has unlimited faith in the corporation. But he writes that:

---

8.   *Ibid*, 54. Original emphasis.

> [I]t is quite possible that whatever we attempt to do in the future will be influenced by corporations, which not only are the chief bearers and generators of technology but the chief sources of jobs, wealth and hope for material well-being. If our families or churches fail, civil society will also fail, and many people will die as a result (73).

The essay requires a more adequate doctrine of the cross and suffering. Corporations can become sinful, corrupt and demonic but they 'can become instruments of preservation and creativity . . . occasions of grace' (70). How? Through our hope in God.

Stackhouse wrote in 1995; I am writing in 2005 when his following words of 1995 now seem somewhat ominous:

> These developments have today brought us to a new, more direct encounter with the great world religions—especially Hinduism, Buddhism, Confucianism, and Islam—which represent the most important, powerful, and profound representations of alternative religions and ethical systems that have ever been able to form enduring civilizations. These are much greater, and much more serious challengers to Christianity than fascism or communism precisely because they more nearly approximate the overt, principled universalism present in religious potentialities and have shown a capacity to organize large and enduring civilizations on these grounds (72).

To set forth the project's rationale it would be best, first of all, to examine Stackhouse's foundational book *Ethics and the*

Urban Ethos[9] where his fundamental thinking is to be found. We will examine his theological evaluation of the megalopolis.

The nature of God in the first half of the book seems Unitarian. 'God' is a symbol (73). However, in the latter half of the book a trinitarian development is made (112), which proves, however, only to be a subtext. The Trinity relates the one God to the many pieties (115). The persons of the Trinity are never inter-related.

He writes that '[t]he doctrine of the Trinity means that the ultimate meta-ethical model must be pluralistic, but it must have a coherence that does not allow the parts to fly into fragmented pluralism' (119). The Trinity supplies 'tools' for ethical reconstruction (142). There is an historical discussion of the fourth and fifth centuries CE regarding the Trinity. But in the end the Trinity, like the kingdom, is but a symbol (193) and a stage along the journey.

The fundamental thought of this book concerns 'power and worth'.[10]

Only in the last sentence of the book does Stackhouse reveal that '(ultimate) worth and power' is to be identified with God:

> But to see the ultimate questions that are at stake . . . and to organize one's projects, thought and group formation around this realization, with all this entails in terms of reordering human priorities, is an act of obedience to that which alone is of ultimate power and worth—God (200, *ad fin*).

Stackhouse does not say that we should worship[11] or say what would accrue to the city if we did, nor is 'ultimate worth

---

9. *Ethics and the Urban Ethos: An Essay in Social Theory and Theological Reconstruction* (Boston: Beacon Press, 1972). Citations are in the body of the text.
10. See pages 73, 88, 92, 94, 107, 108, 117, 118, 127, 132, 134, 136, 137, 139, 141, 142, 152, 154, 155, 158, 161, 165, 169, 171, 172, 175, 184, 185, 187, 189, 190, 191, 192, 197, 198, 200.

and power' brought into play for ordering the ethics of the city. Is worth and power still, really unitarian, or is this reality incarnate in the city?

The book, *God and Globalization: Theological Ethics and the Spheres of Life,* the brain-child of Max Stackhouse, was a project sponsored by the Center of Theological Inquiry, Princeton, New Jersey 1999–2001, although the planning for it began in 1997. The project consisted of four volumes: 'Religion and the Powers of the Common Life' was published in 2000, 'The Spirit and the Modern Authorities', in January 2001, and 'Christ and the Dominions of Civilization' in 2002.[12] My estimation is that the bulk of the work of the project would have been done before mid-2001, a few months before 9/11. Then a bomb was lobbed into the playground of the American theological ethicists on September 11, 2001. The fourth volume on Christian themes and the covenant has not appeared and is not on the horizon.

Here is how Stackhouse begins: 'It is a great delight to introduce these four volumes. Working with one of the finest teams of Christian scholars ever assembled to address one of the most fateful clusters of issues for our time is a demanding joy'. (1:1). This is too precious. In another example of preciosity he writes that '[f]ortunately we have a wonderful team of scholars to do so [to unravel globalism and give all the ability to cope with it]' (3:36).

We come to the matter of a definition of globalisation. Early in the introduction to these three volumes Stackhouse names a hurdle he will have to overcome: 'To many, globalization has nothing to do with religion, theology, or ethics except in changing the way they used to live' (1:5). Another description of globalisation signals the need for the theological ethicist to be active: 'In an emerging global civilization, theological-ethical issues are . . . unavoidable . . . [W]e must come to an informed judgment, as many traditions would put it, about how God wants us to live in the global civilization, to respond to it and to

---

11.   Stackhouse's only mention of worship is: 'Theology is . . . the critical and systematic study of that which man worships' (73).
12.   The volumes were published by Trinity Press International, Harrisburg, Pennsylvania in 2000, 2001, 2002.

shape it' (1:7). But why is it a province of theological ethics? Later on he gives an extremely general description of globalisation: 'The contemporary term "globalization" combines the notions of a worldwide, ordered place of habitation subject to trans-formation' (1:22).

A little later on, Stackhouse opines that globalisation is forming a new 'super-ethos', 'a new comprehending context that owes its allegiance to no particular society, local ethos,or political order, even if it is advanced by "Western influences". (1:19). The impression is given that globalisation—and what is globalised—is a transcendent almost metaphysical reality like the kingdom of God! He argues that many people may think it an evil thing and resist 'globalism as our forebears did facism or communism' (1:19).

Certainly globalisation is a massive threat.

> But since the powers of globalization have largely escaped the control of any society and since religion is the only normative force able to shape and interpret them, it becomes critical for us to compare and contrast the ways in which the various religions are likely to shape persons and societies, to structure the interaction of the complex spheres of life, to aid humanity, and to form a moral response to globalizing conditions (3:35–6).

On whether globalisation is caused by capitalism, Stackhouse takes two contradictory points of view. On the one hand:

> [I]t was in the West generally and in American particularly, deeply stamped by centuries of Christianity, that developments fomenting contemporary forms of capitalism and, this, globalization, were nurtured (1:20). [And it is] a manifestation of the most rapacious, possessive, commodification of the world at the hands of an

unfettered capitalism that is destroying the environment (3:52).

On the other hand he agrees with words of Judith Berling:

> ATS [American Theological Society] schools distance themselves from the Western capitalistic juggernaut sometimes identified with global-ization as in the charge from some . . . that globalization is just another form of Westernization (1:30).

For Stackhouse globalisation is the decisive form of postmodernity (3:21), and we are creating utopia through globalisation (1:8).

But, so far, Stackhouse has not given us a definition of globalisation. He pinches one from Held, McGrew, Goldblatt and Parrator:

> a process (or set of processes) which embodies a transformation in the spatial organization of social relations are transactions—assessed in terms of their extensity, intensity, velocity, and impact—generating transcontinental or inter-regional flows and networks of activity, inter-actions, and the exercise of power (3:4).

This is as good as we are going to get. (Stackhouse could have paid more attention to Roland Robertson, 'Globalization and the Future of "Traditional Religion"' (1:53-68), especially: '[G]lobalization may be defined simply as the compression of the world' (53), but here he does not mention the specific inter-relations of culture, economics and political power—nor the information technology revolution. Nor does anything we have seen so far indicate that globalisation is expressly a movement of these elements which have arisen from the US into global dimension (see 1:8 note, as an afterthought).

Although it goes unacknowledged, Stackhouse's thought is marked by the theology of Tillich (1:10, 1:12, 1:13, 1:16, 1:25,

1:43, 3:18, 3:23). For example 'One indispensable task . . . is to interpret the social contexts of life at the *deepest* moral and spiritual levels' (1:10, emphasis added). And, 'Religions endure by their capacity to provide ultimate meaning . . . ' (1:25).

Still on theology, he stresses the power of the word (communication) but also—in the same breath—natural law and the common good, as though Karl Barth had never existed (1:18). But Stackhouse purports to dislike philosophy (1:2) and privileges theological ethics over theology (1:7). What then can theological ethics do?

> Our indispensable task . . . demands close attention to the work of historians, social scientists, and skilled professionals in other areas. *Theological ethicists* seldom become specialists in a single discipline related to these areas of study, analysis, practice, or reflection, although it is impossible today to do good work in theological ethics without drawing on the research and experience of these fields . . . ethicists want to know, at the deeper levels of motivation and commitment, what sustains the values and norms when they are thwarted, violated, or denied by contrary forces . . . The theological ethicist will enquire into the explicit or implicit view of what is holy, sacred, or inviolable about values and norms and the ethos of a practice, institution, sphere of society, culture or civilization . . . the attempt to do theological ethics presumes that it is possible to evaluate and access, comparatively and critically, both the values and norms of an ethos and the views of what is holy, sacred, or inviolable as these views legitimate a particular ethos, beyond the task of indicative or descriptive discernment (1:9–11. Emphasis added).

It seems that not only is a theological ethicist a man for all seasons, but he or she has, also, the human tools for every situation. According to Stackhouse theological ethics has three tasks: 1) discovering what norms there are whether healthy or whole, 2) assessing what is or ought to be, and 3) a prescriptive task.

Stackhouse posits principalities and powers, authorities, regencies and dominions as aspects of the common life and the common good. This thought has its genesis in the 'principalities and powers' of scripture (Eph 3:10, Col 1:16). These are aspects of life which are immanent to the swirl, course and history of life: 'a cluster of practices and institutions . . . operate to keep these powers functional, ordered, and effective. Each power has also developed, in modernity, a "discipline" by which it is studied, cultivated, and extended' (1:36). These forces will be the organising feature of the four volumes for they are the features of globalisation (1:36). They are spiritual energies in the common life, but not without their negative aspect: 'it is equally impossible to deny that moral and spiritual forces influence life for better or for worse' (1:31). This at the beginning of Stackhouse's discussion of the principalities and powers. Muslims also are 'empowered to fight the principalities and dominions of life that humans have constructed on the basis of their false speculations . . .' (3:54). So, for Stackhouse the principalities and powers are humanly constructed and immanent to the human course of life.

Referring to these principalities, Stackhouse writes as a conclusion to volume one that:

> in the context of the emerging global civilization, and not only in terms of archaic and pervasive spiritual energies or the modern social sciences, but also in terms of basic theological and ethical questions as they relate to our globalizing world. Are these principalities built into the structure of creation and thus part of the intent of the Creator? Are they given by God? If so are they operating in accord with the divine intent, in recognition of the reality and depths of broken-ness that attends existence? Or are the prin-cipalities so disordered or distorting that we must abandon them, or suffer their slow destruction

with resistance and passive regret? Can they be
redeemed or must they be avoided? Above all,
how can, how ought such issues be discussed in
public discourse? (1:44-5).

If Stackhouse cannot make up his mind, how will his readers
fare?

And so aspects of our common life 'are held to be holy and
divine or of transcendent worth' (3:6).

On the basis of Ephesians 3:10 I would hold that the
'principalities and powers' are indeed transcendent realities of a
largely negative nature. For Stackhouse they are merely
immanent to the life of humanity, society and civilisation,
whereas in scripture they are transcendental, capable of
wreaking metaphysical evil on the civilisation of human beings.
His immanence means that Stackhouse cannot deal with evil
and sin. Where is Christ Pantocrator (Philip 2:5–11; Col 2:8–15)
to deal with the principalities and powers (see 2:36)? There is a
dualism between the transcendent and the immanent in
Stackhouse's treatment of the 'principalities and powers' and he
is really plumbing the latter.

There are five faces of the principalities, powers, dominions,
authorities and regencies: Mammon, Mars, Eros, the Muses and
Religion (1:37–9) which are foci of common life and are found in
every society.

So religion is just one of the features of the common life. But
Stackhouse can schematise the five faces and their dominions
and expansively outline religion without mentioning Christ
(2:14).

According to Stackhouse every society has its heroes (though
here is no mention of Joseph Campbell and his myths). This
topic is signalled suddenly near the end of the second volume
(2:36), and Jesus is just one of the gang:

> every society and culture has had its heroes and
> great philosophical and religious figures. Moses,
> Jesus, Augustine, Thomas, Luther and Calvin of
> course, but also Plato, Aristotle, the Buddha,
> ankara, Ramanuja, Confucius, Ming, Tzu,

Mohammed, and Maimonides, for example have
attracted attention across several societies and
cultures, serving not only as heroes of faith and
learning, but as personal exemplars and moral
role models. In most traditions, the roster of
saints is long' (1:48).

This is an arbitrary grab bag and where are the women?!
Stackhouse's syncretism is evident in the following:

> [T]o speak of the 'Lord Jesus Christ' is socially
> and religiously similar in an analytic or structural
> way to what can be found in the devotion to the
> Spirit Elders of the tribes, to the Lords Krishna,
> Ram, or Visnu among the Hindus, or that toward
> the Lord Buddha, the Prophet and Model
> Muhammad [sic] and the Sage Confucius [and]
> are said to point by those who follow them.
> Moreover, those who claim Jesus Christ as Lord
> must recognise that those who have followed
> other lords have generated distinctive ways of
> organizing the principalities and powers of the
> common life . . . (3:18).

It should be remembered in passing that Stackhouse never
mentions what is probably the most distinctive aspect of
Christianity: the Incarnation of Jesus Christ. The closest he
comes to it is stating the 'presupposition that a coherent *logos*
stands behind all of existence and history' (3:26).

In view of the above, why has Stackhouse left us with this
open-ended question at the end of volume 2? 'Our question will
be [presumably for subsequent volumes] whether Christ is, can
be, and should become Lord over all the powers, principalities,
authorities, and regencies in a global civilization' (2:36).

In Lamin Sanneh's essay, 'Muhammad in Muslim Tradition
and Practice: The Crucible of Faith and the Spheres of
Dominion' (3:272–308), the prophet takes on distinctly christological features. Stackhouse comments that 'Lamin Sanneh
explores the ways in which Mohammed [sic] is not only seen as

the fulfilling prophet of the Abrahamic, Jewish, and Christian traditions, but also plays the role of social model' (1:51).

Stackhouse addresses the Chinese situation (3:42–5), and notes that Confucianism and communist ideology have lost their hold on the people. At the same time religion is influencing the people in China in a renaissance, most visibly in Falun Gong (about which the Chinese leadership has 'apoplexy' as Stackhouse puts it). Further, there are other forms such as evangelical, pentecostal groups and house churches, as well as the 'underground church', the Roman Catholic bishops (as opposed to state appointed Catholic bishops), and their flocks who are mostly constrained by the communist leadership. Stackhouse's summary is that the Chinese lack an 'inner Lord' in their society and common life. However, Stackhouse is too optimistic in the following: 'Yet globalization, in which China is one of the most recent and authentic participants, is bringing all the pressures to form . . . a civil society' (3:43).

Volume 3 is largely about the world religions. Confuciansm is dealt with in 3:42–5, Hinduism in 3:47–8, the Religions of the Book 3:52, Buddhism 3:49, 51, 53 and Islam 3:49, 52–55. Discussions between the religions are broached (3:34, 35).

Here are his introductory remarks about Islam among the 'Religions of the Book':

> Islam, which has the most strict view of divine revelation of any of the great religions . . . and it is different from Christianity, which has a profound understanding of divine inspiration but acknowledges the role of human insight and authorship in both their discernment of truth and the actualization of justice. This latter position, common to Judaism and Christianity, has a twofold implication. It suggests that ultimate truth and justice are simultaneously transcendent and intimately present in the time, space, and flesh of life, and that whatever we can come to know about them must be both disclosed and received, observed and enacted—lovingly incarnated in earthen vessels (3:52).

In this, as so often, Stackhouse strains for the sublime and the earthy at the same time, starts with a point that he then fully (or partly) negates and ends up with almost a cartoon of what is the actual situation.

Some prescient remarks are made about Islam by Stackhouse and it is worthwhile stating them in full:

> [I]t is quite possible that . . . [Islam] will have a greater influence in the global future, post challenges to and interact dramatically with Christianity, and, in some ways, serve as potentially great allies and simultaneously possible great enemies of the globalizing forces that were primarily launched out of an ethos shaped by Christianity (3:49).

> Islam . . . poses direct challenges to the prospects of globalization insofar as this process is generating the material infrastructure for a pluralist global civil society. It is itself a globalizing religion, and some historians argue that its rootage in the drive to overcome the fractious conflicts of tribal and clan hostilities of the earlier pagan polytheism of the old Mideast gave rise to a universalizing warrior cult of intense discipline that must fulfill its destiny by unifying the world and establishing a universal reign under a single law. But this is not how Muslims understand their origin. The profound rootage of this tradition is explicitly not found in observation but in revelation—in fact with a basic theory of revelation that is often called in the West 'fundamentalism' when it is applied to the Bible. This view holds that a transcendent personal God revealed His will, in teachings and commands, which were inerrantly spoken to Muhammad, recited by him and recorded by inspired scribes. This is the resource for knowing universal truths that we ought to study and obey

without remainder. When we submit to this true
Lord, as so known, we are called to spread the
truth that is now finally and fully available,
empowered to fight the *principalities and
dominions* of life that humans have constructed
on the basis of their false speculations, and
promised an immediate place in paradise if we
faithfully carry out our duties or die in the effort
(3:53–4. Emphasis added).

Once again Stackhouse is such a scarlet pimpernel that it is
very difficult to tell (a) what he is actually saying, and (b) what
his own views are.

However, that having been said, he was prescient that Islam
posed a threat—even to his own project: 'If Islam becomes the
dominant force in guiding the globalization process, it will take
the process in a very different direction than now appears to be
the trajectory' (3:55). And then came 9/11.

Stackhouse has a slight eschatology. He seems to hope that
the future will bring more answers than he has now, and that
the eschaton would bring the solutions of all things.

Apart from Stackhouse himself, one of the greatest casualties
in these three volumes of 9/11 seems to be David Tracy who
wrote the essay 'Public Theology, Hope, and the Mass Media:
Can the Muses Still Inspire?' (1:231–254) for the first volume
which must have been written at the latest in 1999. He then
flags two forthcoming books, *On Naming and Thinking God* and
The Side of God which have not appeared at the late date of July
2005.

There is no admission in these three introductions that
globalisation is an economic/political/military thrust of the
United States to the heart of the globe.

Stackhouse says that the design of the total project and
volumes was his own (1:1).

Max Lynn Stackhouse is such a mercurial (thinker and)
writer that I have had to quote verbatim large amounts of his
writings so as to tease out what is actually being said by the
general editor of *God and Globalization*.

Augustine and Globalisation[1]

According to Augustine's reckoning there are two realities: the city of God (or the heavenly city), and the earthly city.

The earthly city is created by the lust for domination (*libido dominandi*) over others in which there is a 'swelling of pride (*superbia*)' or exercise of sheer power by the person or group concerned.

> We see that sin was brought on through pride (*superbia*) . . . such that they refused to be under

---

1.   The best biography of Augustine is: Peter RL Brown, *Augustine of Hippo* (Berkeley and Los Angeles: University of California Press, 1967). For a thumb-nail sketch see Henry Chadwick, *The Church in Ancient Society: From Galilee to Gregory the Great* (Oxford: Oxford University Press, 2000), 473–478. See also Eleonore Stump and Norman Kretzmann (editors) *The Cambridge Companion to Augustine* (Cambridge: Cambridge University Press, 2001). That Augustine was a great Christian thinker was known even in his own time. Jerome writes to Augustine, Ep 195, 418 CE: 'You are known throughout the world; Catholics honor and esteem you as the one who has established anew the ancient faith; and, what is a mark of greater glory, all the heretics denounce you'.

       See also: Charles Norris Cochrane, *Christianity and Classical Culture: A Study of Thought and Action from Augustus to Augustine* (Oxford: Oxford University Press, 1940); RA Markus, *Saeculum: History and Society in the Theology of St Augustine* (Cambridge: Cambridge University Press, 1970); John Neville Figgis, *The Political Aspects of St Augustine's 'City of God'* (Gloucester, Mass: Peter Smith, 1963 [1921]); Oliver O'Donovan, *The Problem of Self-Love in St Augustine* (New Haven: Yale University Press, 1980); Herbert A Deane, *The Political and Social Ideas of St Augustine* (New York: Columbia University Press, 1963); William S Babcock (editor) *The Ethics of St Augustine* (Atlanta, Georgia: Scholars Press, 1991); GR Evans, *Augustine on Evil* (Cambridge: Cambridge University Press, 1982); Charles T Mathewes, *Evil and the Augustinian Tradition* (Cambridge: Cambridge University Press, 2001); RW Dyson, *The Pilgrim City: Social and Political Ideas in the Writings of St Augustine of Hippo* (Woodbridge: The Boydell Press, 2001); EM Atkins and RJ Dodaro, *Augustine: Political Writings* (Cambridge: Cambridge University Press, 2001); Augustine, *City of God*, edited by David Knowles, translated by Henry Bettenson (Harmondsworth: Penguin, 1972).

God (*sub Deo*) but [preferred] to be in their own power without the Lord (*in sua potestate potius sine Domino*) . . . as though God were jealous lest they ruled themselves (*ne se ipse regerent*) . . . Thus they were persuaded, therefore, to love their own power to excess (*ut suam potestatem nimis amarent*), and since they wished to be God's equals, they put to bad use that mid-rank character (*medietas*) whereby subject to God, they held bodies in subject to themselves . . . (*Genesis Against the Manichees* 11.22).

At the root of the two cities are two loves, the love of self which we have just described as the 'earthly city' and the love of God which is the 'heavenly city' or city of God. *Verus philosophus est amator Dei*, 'the true philosopher is the lover of God' (*The City of God* VIII.1). 'Knowledge puffs up, love builds up' (1 Cor 8:1).

This is worship, the ultimate worship of ourselves for God, on one hand, and the arrogant worship of self or the pomp of this world and all its glory in this world on the other hand. The love of God in the 'City of God' springs from humility.

This may all be seen in the early pages of the Old Testament. Cain lusted for domination so he murdered Abel—as Romulus killed Remus to found the Roman Empire.

Original sin came into being through the fall of Adam and Eve, and the 'earthly city' always arises from the original sin of man and woman. This may always be seen in their affairs.

Behind all is the predestination of God.

Power is unfailingly the function of pride and for that reason it is unstable; empires are formed and empires deteriorate and fall. The 'earthly city' is divided against itself. The love of God, the love for and worship of God on the other hand, which forms 'the heavenly city', or city of God, is stable and leads to the kingdom of God which is ultimately an eschatological entity.

In life and history it is difficult to distinguish the two cities for in the reality of life they are, as Augustine put it, 'mixed'. The state is not as such the earthly city. The state and the political and legal order, as Deane put it, have 'remedial functions'.

> The State has an important coercive function over against the 'earthly city' to contain its operations within limits and discipline it. Coercion can be great or small.[2]

What I have set out above is Augustine's exposition in *The City of God* which he wrote as a theodicy to justify Christianity and the church and Godafter Alaric the Visigoth sacked 'eternal' Rome in 410 CE.

Augustine's pessimism about earthly realities can be found, for example, in *The City of God*:

> Remove justice, and what are Kingdoms but gangs of criminals on a large scale? And what are criminal gangs but petty Kingdoms? (IV.4).

The state's ostensible aim is justice; no justice can naturally be found in the 'earthly city'. Justice is the core reality (*iustitia*) of the *City of God*.

Thus Augustine is realistic about the state and argues against the views of the state found in Aristotle and Cicero who saw it as a completely positive reality in and through which people's life is well formed: 'The state comes into being so that men may live. It remains in being so that they may live well' (Aristotle, *Politics* 1278b 20–30).

There is *superbia* here as well: '[p]ride is the craving for undue exaltation' (*City of God* XIV: 10–14) 'the cause of all human offences'. 'You cannot, therefore, attribute the cause of any human fault to God; for the cause of all human offences is pride.' (Of the meriting and remission of sins II:17–27). So we cannot overestimate the origin, facility, omnipresence, and effect of pride.

In the final analysis the 'city of God' is always a pilgrimage in this life (*civitas Dei peregrina*) and the institutional church

---

2.   Deane, *op cit*, 78.

cannot be simply identified with it, indeed the 'city of God' in its eschatological reality is pure and more ultimate. The end of the city of God, eschatologically, is salvation; that of the earthly city is damnation.

In sum, then: the state is inveterately rooted in and associated with sin. It arises from sin; it institutionalises sinful impulses of envy, aggression and acquisition; and the claim of Rome, or of any other state, to embody more than an approximate and instrumental kind of justice is simply false. The state is not a moral community; it is not a polis of the kind made familiar to us by Plato and Aristotle.[3] When, therefore, death shall be swallowed up in victory, these things shall not be there; and there shall be peace—peace full and eternal. We shall be in a kind of city. [The city of God]. 'Brethren, when I speak of that city, and especially when scandals grow great here, I just cannot bring myself to stop' (*Exposition of the Psalms* LXXXIV.10).

Augustine's is not as bleak a view of social and political reality as that of Thomas Hobbes. Augustine has had a marked influence on many: including John Milbank, *Theology and Social Theory*, and Hannah Arendt, *The Origins of Totalitarianism*.[4]

---

3.   Dyson, *op cit*, 57.

4.   Thomas Hobbes, *Leviathan* (Harmondsworth: Penguin, 1968). John Milbank, *Theology and Social Theory: Beyond Secular Reason* (Oxford: Blackwell, 1990). Hannah Arendt, *The Origins of Totalitarianism* (New York: A Harvest Book, Harcourt Brace and Company, 1979).

Globalisation: A Critique

Globalisation is an economic phenomenon with political ramifications whereby economic and political aspects of the world become predicated of the whole world itself. Central to it is a spirit of competition, by which the world is globalised and results in a sense of one globe.

This has a similarity in many ways to what we know as empire. To assist an understanding of globalisation I will trace the church's experience of empire. Karl Rahner saw three eras of the church: 1) the apostolic, 2) the european, and 3) the global.

The church's experience of empire began with the history of the people of God in Scripture, with its experience of the Assyrian, Babylonian, Persian, Greek and Roman empires. During the conflict with the Assyrian empire in the eighth century BCE the ten northern tribes were taken away and never heard of again.

The Babylonian empire succeeded the Assyrian empire and in the sixth century took the two Southern tribes of Judah away to Babylonian captivity. Then the Persian might overcame Babylon and Cyrus the Persian King allowed the people of God to return to Palestine under Ezra and Nehemiah after approximately fifty years of captivity. Yahweh even calls Cyrus 'his anointed' (Isa 45:1).

Israel weathered far better the remnants of Alexander the Great's Greek empire and the Roman empire up until the fall of Jerusalem in 70 CE.

These empires were economic and political entities. Each had a vision of itself as the globe at that time (its worldview) and anything else that was not naturally part of this was subsumed under its reality and became part of it. Each was an economic, political and military operation. From time to time a new empire would arise and engulf the old one.

Further critical examination of these situations is likely to give us information about how the people of God not only would fare in an imperial situation, but also in globalisation.

The assumption of globalisation is that there is one globe to dominate.

The Christian assumption is different: that there is one God, and so one world, and a heavenly world beyond. This is taught beginning with Old Teastament Scripture. 'The Lord our God is one lord . . .' (Deut 6:4). The Pauline epistles posit one cosmos or world. Christ died for *all*. And the unity of all things, under the one God in the New Testament faith is seen in 'one Lord, one faith, one baptism' (Eph 4:5).

Hitherto there has been little ability to realise this one world. The missionary endeavours of the church, both ancient and modern, bore this in mind. In the early period (third century CE), there was strong expansion of the church despite persecutions like the Diocletian and the Decian, to the situation where the church could not be resisted and there was a settlement under Constantine.

In the later period, wherever empire went the church went over the globe. It does not matter whether the mercantilist power was Spain, Portugal, Holland or Britain. In each case the church could hardly be distinguished from the imperial power. When the imperial powers became privately owned economic juggernauts, the missionary churches continued but felt a little lost. Their acute minds realised that again the church was in a counter-cultural situation.

The problem with this outcome was that the churches seemed content simply to be an x, y and z and be the church there, in the mercantilist situation and forgetting about God's one world.

From the beginning the church had been counter-cultural. This put Christ on the cross, and impelled the church around the Roman Empire. Its evangelism was against the situation of the day in the name of salvation and justice. So naturally the church was persecuted and it was only when the authorities realised the church could not be persecuted out of existence that Christianity was made a licenced religion (*religio licita*) by the Emperor Constantine in the early fourth century CE.

The Constantinian settlement is the greatest example of the church's positive relation to the state. It ceased to be a counter-cultural religion. It was established.

All these are examples of the church's relationship to empire. Being one Body of Christ in one cosmos, is it always to be in conflict with empire as in Scripture or at one with it as with Constantine and to a lesser extent with the mercantilist powers?

The twentieth century, like the nineteenth century before it, has been the period of the empire. The Austro-Hungarian, German, Russian and British empires were embroiled in the Great War. Then Italian fascism, and Nazi Germany grew up and were involved with the British empire, Japan, the Soviet Union and the United States in the Second World War. After World War Two we had the Cold War with two empires facing each other: Soviet Russia and the United States. Since the Soviet Union disintegrated in 1991, with Gorbachev's assistance, there has been only one empire: the American. Now the question is whether there are two opposing forces: Christian civilisation and Islamic civilisation.

In each conflict it has been about the mastery of the globe.

Globalisation now means economic realities which begin in the United States.

In the twentieth century the church has begun to realise its 'oneness' in the 'oneness' of the world in the ecumenical movement. This is not enough. If the church is really to address one world and the forces of globalisation that would take over the world, it must become really 'one'. Previously the church has moved when the culture has moved, now the church must move before the culture. The infinitesimal movement of the church toward unity in the disunity and conflict of the world must become a real movement of 'oneness' and wholeness.

Only this will address the world in an age of globalisation.

The capitalist economic forces which are vying for the world in globalisation are religious in origin and probably in form (see Max Weber's *The Protestant Ethic and the Spirit of Capitalism*, [1904–5]). So it is Christianity's task to be both counter-cultural as she always has been and accommodating as in the Constantinian settlement.

For a moment I had a vision of a world that seemed to wear a vast and dismal aspect of disorder, while, in truth, thanks to our unwearied efforts, it is as sunny an arrangement of small conveniences as the mind of man can conceive.

Joseph Conrad, *Lord Jim.*

Globalisation and Empire

Without realising that they were walking on a globe, they walked further and further away from each other, passed the equator and started to meet again. It is that meeting we call in our day and age 'globalisation'.[1]

In this chapter I wish to outline the ideas of a number of authors on globalisation.

I

Australian author, Keith Suter, introduces the topic of globalisation in the following manner:

The new era is 'global', rather than 'international'. The word 'international' regards the country (or 'nation-state') as the basic building block of world affairs so that 'international co-operation' means governments working together. However, the new global era recognises that there are other actors on the world stage and that nation-states and their national governments no longer have a monopoly of power.[2]

Traditionally, 'globalisation' has been meant economic globalisation which:

refers to the transnational corporations and the creation of a consumption-dominated global middle class. Unlike a century ago when there were fewer consumer goods available, now there

---

1. JG Donders, 'Summa Theologiae', *Eureka Street* vol 14 no 3 (April 2004): 9.
2. Keith Suter, *In Defence of Globalisation* (Sydney: University of New South Wales Press, 2000), 9.

is virtually a limitless choice of goods and services.[3]

Suter wants rather to emphasise public order globalisation and popular globalisation to make sure that 'globalisation as a whole works for the benefit of ordinary people and not just the wealthy few'.[4] He wants to describe these two as the following:

1. 'Public order globalization' refers to governments having to work together on common problems, such as combating disease and protecting the environment. This is often done through inter-governmental organisations such as the United Nations and the European Union.[5]
2. 'Popular globalization' refers to the campaigns by people power organisations, such as Amnesty International and Greenpeace. These organisations are able to use information technology and the mass media to assist their campaigns, such as the demonstrations against the World Trade Organisation in Seattle at the end of 1999.[6]

So, at the outset it would seem Suter is pitting himself against hard-core globalisation or globalisation as it has been known, prosecuted by the few and opposed (and misunderstood) by the many. He argues that 'the challenge is to find ways of coping with globalisation—the clock cannot be turned back to the more stable and secure world of the 1950s. We need to find ways of making lemonade out of this lemon.'[7]

The nation-state, Suter suggests, had been the building blocks of the world from the Peace of Westphalia in 1648:

---

3.   *Ibid.*
4.   *Ibid.*
5.   *Ibid.*
6.   *Ibid.*
7.   *Ibid*, 10

> The nation-state system is . . . not a fixed fact of political life, as nationalists like to claim. It has been created by humans in the last 350 years. The system began in Europe and it was taken around the world by the European imperialists as they carved up Africa, Asia and the other regions. When the European colonies became independent, they stayed with the system rather than revert to their old systems, such as tribal ones, and they retained the national borders imposed upon them by the imperialists.[8]

These nation-states in Europe asserted themselves against trans-national realities like the papacy, monastic and knightly orders. Nationhood and national identity were necessary myths for the purposes of foreign policy. Natural law and the Medieval internationalism had been replaced.

'In nation-states', Suter writes, 'positivism replaced the natural law. "Positivism" meant that laws were to be based solely on "facts" and decisions from governments.'[9]

International treaties could be accepted or foregone. And the concept of sovereignty evolved from absolute monarchs in the older Europe, to a toned down centrality of one person after the American and French revolutions.

Suter argues in his book 'that the world is moving into a post-Westphalian era, with the globalisation process creeping up on the nation-states'.[10]

The real force for unity in the second half of the twentieth century was the 'transnational corporations . . . knitting the world together' surreptitiously while the politicians and military were preparing for World War III and fighting conventional wars.[11] The latter became an irrelevancy. 'A transnational corporation is a company that engages in foreign direct

---

8.   *Ibid*, 15.
9.   *Ibid*, 16.
10. *Ibid*, 18.
11. *Ibid*, 19.

investment and owns (or controls) activities in more than one country'.[12]

He goes on to argue that:

> Transnational corporations are now the main global economic force and have eroded the ability of the nation to have an economic economy. Transnational corporations sprawl across national political boundaries and cut in different ways to maximise profits.[13]

So, for Sutter, 'national governments no longer have much control over their economies'.[14] Therefore, full employment can no longer be ensured and the marketing that ordinary people were accustomed to two centuries ago of knowing the people you bought from and selling them your goods face to face has gone. For instance, you simply drive to the supermarket. 'Consumerism is the leading edge of the globalised economy.'[15] We do not buy things because we *need* them but because it is *beyond* your life and *'enhances'* it. We *need* very little.

Because of the Westphalian system of nation-states the states are, unfortunately, entitled to have nothing to do with an international Court of Justice.[16]

> The final and most fascinating example of 'co-operation' [over the world] is the internet. It was conceived in 1964 as a computer network that had thousands of links but no governing authority, on which messages travelled randomly. This was a response to US worries about the Cold War and the threat of a surprise nuclear attack on it. If the United States' surface were attacked and telephone lines were destroyed, the

---

12.   *Ibid.*
13.   *Ibid.*
14.   *Ibid*, 20.
15.   *Ibid*, 21.
16.   *Ibid*, 28.

senior officers would need a system that could not be disrupted. Thus the Internet evolved and just kept on growing. It is creating new opportunities for friendship and co-operation around the world. It has also been a useful campaigning tool for non-governmental organizations . . . Ironically, many of the rallies against economic globalisation are now being co-ordinated through the Internet.[17]

Suter believes in 'people power'; he is positive and confident that NGOs (non-government organisations) can be used by people across the world for a better future (chapter 4, 35–41).

However, Keith Suter is too naïve about globalisation:

There is no doubt that the future belongs to globalisation because the process has moved too far too fast to be stopped now . . . while there may be widespread opposition to globalisation, promoted through certain religious and political extremists or other interest groups, the fact is people . . . want consumer items . . . [18]

It would appear that, in the end, Suter is on the side of hard core economic globalisation after all.

Suter speaks of the 'politics of anger' of those who do not understand [enlightenment model?] who are favourites of uncomprehending voters. He speaks of people like right wing Australian politician, Pauline Hanson, and France's Jean LePen.

Politicians tend to tell people what they want to hear, rather than what they need to know. What people have needed to know is that the process of globalisation is underway, traditional ideas of the role of national government are no longer relevant, and that there is a limited capacity for

17. *Ibid*, 31.
18. *Ibid*, 42.

any such government to do much to slow the overall pace of global change.[19]

Suter has a far too optimistic view of the United Nations in global terms which allows him to be utterly pessimistic about nation states and national governments.

The people are to blame:

> This is the era of the survival of the glibbest . . . If people paid as much attention to globalisation as they did to the performance of their local sporting team, then they would not have been taken by surprise by the process of globalisation.[20]

However, 'national governments will not disappear in the new global era but they will have to adjust to a new role'.[21]

So, we are faced with a post-democratic society,[22] or are we?

Suter returns to his original point: 'there is the challenge of ensuring that economic globalisation works for the benefit of more people'.[23]

Finally, Suter makes some ad hoc suggestions about how ordinary people might live with the trans-national corporations: 'boycotts, girlcotts, buying goods made under just working conditions, investment guidelines, socially responsible investment and investing in corporations in which you disapprove [sic] so as to change their policies'.[24] Is that all? Surely Suter meant to write: investing in corporations which you ethically approve so as to change the policies of corporations with which you disapprove?! One gets the impression that Suter thinks the situation is almost irretrievable.

---

19.   *Ibid*, 44.
20.   *Ibid*, 46.
21.   *Ibid*, 49.
22.   *Ibid*, 50.
23.   *Ibid*, 53.
24.   *Ibid*, 54.

II

Another Australian contribution, fostered by the Evatt Foundation in Sydney, is *Globalisation: Australian Impacts*. The book is edited by Christopher Sheil, with a number of significant contributions on a range of topics and themes.[25]

Sheil rejects that globalisation is inevitable and that globalisation and the nation-state are necessarily opposed. The book was being completed as Australia celebrated its centenary of Federation in January 2001. The editor writes that 'The organisation of this book commenced in 1998. In the meantime, much has happened to diminish the triumphalism then associated with globalisation.'

Sheil argues that globalisation is more complex than the Australian government allows; the Prime Minister might just as well be speaking in 1788. One contributor, John Quiggin, writes that deregulation can be seen 'as the "re-regulation" of the economy in the interests of global capital'.[26] 'The rise of global financial capital . . . places the issue of public ownership firmly back on the agenda'.[27]

Another contributor, Peter J Rimmer, believes that it is clear that Australian governments have taken divergent approaches to the globalisation of transport systems. He writes that 'in many ways, Australia has been caught in a double bind by a global transport system that is being fashioned to meet the needs of transnational corporations, rather than nation-states'.[28]

In the same volume, Ros Eason, writing on telecommunications, argues that:

> 'Globalisation' is scarcely a new phenomenon, if by that term we simply mean the ongoing restructuring of production and markets and world states under the lash of finance capital . . . Indeed, to penetrate the arcane world of inter-

25.   *Globalisation: Australian Impacts*, edited by Christopher Sheil (Sydney: UNSW Press, 2001).
26.   *Ibid*, 10
27.   *Ibid*, 33
28.   *Ibid*, 54

national accounting rates is to glimpse, in outline,
the trade wars of the information economy.[29]

In another chapter Terry Flew and Stuart Cunningham write
on the role of media outlets arguing that they are:

> central to the globalisation debates, partly
> because of their role as communication tech-
> nologies that enable the international distribution
> of messages and meanings, but mainly because of
> their perceived role in weakening the cultural
> bonds that tie people to nation-states and national
> communities.[30]

As a result, they argue we have McWorld, Coco-colonisation
and Disneyfication of the globe.[31]

Michael Paddon writes on corporations: 'the production of
goods and services in countries that are controlled and
managed by firms headquartered in other countries—that is the
core of the process of globalisation'.[32] He gives an overview of
corporations and assesses the effects of 'deregulation,
privatisation, corporate restructuring and new technologies in
giving impulse to their growth'.[33] Regulation of trans-national
corporations is necessary, difficult but essential.[34]

Patricia Ranald writes about unions, arguing that the
freedom and well-being of the workers is difficult to ensure,
especially in the sub-contracting situation of globalisation.[35]
'Unions cannot match the global reach and strength of trans-
national corporations, but nor are they powerless in the face of
globalisation'.[36]

---

29.   *Ibid*, 63–64.
30.   *Ibid*, 77
31.   *Ibid*, 79
32.   *Ibid*, 97.
33.   *Ibid*, 98.
34.   *Ibid*, 122–23.
35.   *Ibid*, 136.
36.   *Ibid*, 141.

Australian Labor Party politician, the Hon Kevin Rudd, writes on governance. 'The central argument is that '[g]lobalisation] 'is gathering momentum and generating both positive and negative impacts'.[37] '[G]lobalisation is in fact a synonym for Americanisation'.[38] 'Globophobia may constitute a satisfying political response to the complex challenges of globalisation for some, but it does not constitute a credible policy response capable of shaping the actions of governments'.[39]

Roy Green and Andrew Wilson write on industry: '"[G]lobalisation" is just the latest form of neo-liberalism, the major influence over Western capitalism since the 1970s.'[40] But, the new element associated with globalisation is the justification for this agenda; the development of global markets has allegedly undermined the autonomy of the nation state and the possibility of effective controls in capital. They believe that the 'identification of globalisation with free trade is . . . fundamentally misconceived'.[41] 'The outcomes will not be dictated directly in accordance with neo-liberal 'globalisation' ideology, but only in the course of real political struggle',[42] is their final word.

Terri Seddon and Simon Marginson write on education:

> The weakening of the welfare state and income redistribution, plus tax reform, means that the natural tendency of global markets (like all markets) to increase disparities of wealth and power is no longer offset by contrary trends, either national or supranational. The 'lag' between market globalisation and the development of global dominance and global social policies is being strongly felt. There is a growing

---

37. *Ibid*, 151.
38. *Ibid*, 155.
39. *Ibid*, 159.
40. *Ibid*, 166.
41. *Ibid*, 172.
42. *Ibid*, 182.

disparity between rich and poor countries, and
between the rich and poor within each country.[43]

Rai Small writes on health: 'From the neo-liberal perspective,
public regulation and ownership are limitations, and public
health care is portrayed as little more than a crumbling restraint
on globalisation, the advance of which is "inevitable"'.[44]

Deborah Mitchell writes on welfare. She quotes Australian
Prime Minister John Howard (in 1999): '"Globalisation . . . is
creating deep social pain and political costs as sensitive sectors
are opened up to outside competition and go through difficult
adjustments. The human costs are hurtful and governments
have a responsibility to help people through the process.'"[45]

Quentin Beresford writes on rights. He questions if human
rights are the embodiment and driving force of globalisation?[46]
He suggests that we should be sceptical. Lionel Orchard writes
on democracy: that we are 'citizens of the world' has a long and
distinguished history.[47] But is there really a one world?[48]
Democratic policies in politics is in the vernacular of the people
concerned.[49]

In his conclusion Christopher Sheil writes:

> One conclusion is certain in a world that
> continues to shrink in time and space: these
> growing disparities, which are an integral part of
> the present meaning of globalisation, are not only
> morally repugnant and economically wasteful;
> they are also ultimately politically unsus-
> tainable.[50]

---

43.   *Ibid*, 205.
44.   *Ibid*, 223.
45.   *Ibid*, 236.
46.   *Ibid*, 240.
47.   *Ibid*, 267.
48.   *Ibid*, 275.
49.   *Ibid*, 277.
50.   *Ibid*, 287.

'Globalisation means freedom for capital, not freedom from systemic suffering'.[51] The control signifier is 'imperialism'.[52]

It is good to have a small Western country like Australia where its scholars can be so clear-eyed and perceptive about the signs of the times.

III

Pulitzer prize winning columnist for the *New York Times,* Thomas L Friedman, has written *The Lexus and the Olive Tree* on globalisation.[53] Friedman's preface is very instructive.

He suggests that there have been two periods of globalisation in world history. One from the mid 1800's until 1914 and the other from the fall of the Berlin wall until now. The former period was miniscule compared with the latter. The break between the two periods occurred because of the Russian revolution, the two World Wars, the depression and the Cold War. When the last period was over, the full power of American capitalism could be unleashed on the world.

Friedman suggests that writers such as Kaplan, Fukuyama, Huntington and Paul M Kennedy are wrong about the post-1989 situation. He suggests that they think in black and white terms, whereas, although there are positives and negatives to the globalisation situation, it is all to the good and holistic. Indeed he is prepared to talk about 'the brutalities of globalisation', a 'system that can benefit the most people, while inflicting the least amount of pain'.[54]

In opposing Huntington, who propounded the clash of civilisations, Western Christendom and Islam, he writes that we will 'go back to kicking the Hindus and Muslims around and

---

51. *Ibid*, 293.
52. *Ibid*, 295.
53. Thomas L Friedman, *The Lexus and the Olive Tree* (London: Harper Collins, 2000 [1999]). See also Thomas L Friedman, *The World is Flat: A Brief History of the Globalized World in the 21ˢᵗ Century* (Carlton, Vic: Allen Lane, 2005).
54. *Ibid*, xxii.

them kicking us'.[55] Friedman emerges as an ardent globaliser, indeed a gung-ho globaliser.[56]

'Globalization is not just some economic fad, and it is not just a passing trend. It is an international system . . We need to understand it as such.'[57]

The driving force behind globalisation is free-market capitalism. Friedman defines globalisation like this:

> . . . it is the inexorable integration of markets, nation-states and technologies to a degree never witnessed before—in a way that is enabling individuals, corporations and nation-states to reach around the world farther, faster, deeper and cheaper than ever before, and in a way that is enabling the world to reach into individual corporations and nation-states further, faster, deeper, cheaper than ever before.[58]

There is a process of 'creative destruction' in which 'only the paranoid survive' and 'innovation replaces tradition'.[59]

Friedman's Manichaeism, or plain simple dualism, could not be more evident than in the following: 'the world for me was all about watching people clinging to their own roots and uprooting their neighbour's olive trees'.[60] The Middle East is the context of the remark.

Globalisation lacks the pastoral, personal, human touch: 'Global integration has raced ahead of education. Thanks to globalization, we all definitely know "of" one another more than ever, but we still don't know much "about" one another.'[61]

---

55.   *Ibid*, xx-xxi.
56.   *Ibid*, xxi.
57.   *Ibid*, 7.
58.   *Ibid*, 9.
59.   *Ibid*, 11.
60.   *Ibid*, 20.
61.   *Ibid*, 127.

The ethics of globalisation can be challenged: 'For the herd [the financiers who control the system], corruption is just another name for unpredictability'.[62]

This raises the question: what would be an ethics of globalisation? Friedman asks: 'How do we get better global *governance*, in areas such as environment, human rights, financial interactions and work on conditions, without having global government?'[63]

What is Friedman's environmental solution for environmentally sustainable globalisation? 'We need to demonstrate to the herd that being green, being global and being greedy can go hand in hand. If you want to save the Amazon, go to business school and learn how to do a deal.'[64]

For Freidman, the most important 'filter' to globalisation is 'glocalisation'. He defines glocalisation—think global but act locally—in the following manner:

> the ability of a culture, when it encounters other strong cultures, to absorb influences that naturally fit into and can enrich that culture, to resist those things that are truly alien and to compartmentalize those things that, while different, can nevertheless be enjoyed and celebrated as different. The whole purpose of globalizing is to be able to assimilate aspects of globalization into your country and culture in a way that adds to your growth and diversity, without overwhelming it.[65]

Glocalism alone, though he argues, 'even in its most healthy form, is not sufficient to protect indigenous cultures from globalization. Some hard filters are needed'.[66]

---

62. *Ibid*, 180.
63. *Ibid*, 206.
64. *Ibid*, 282-3.
65. *Ibid*, 295.
66. *Ibid*, 297.

IV

The economist Joseph E Stiglitz was chair of President Clinton's Council of Economic Advisors, and subsequently the chief economist at the World Bank.[67] He was a Nobel laureate in economics in 2001. Stiglitz has written *Globalization and its Discontents*.[68]

Stiglitz's time in office made him concerned 'to make globalization more humane, effective and equitable . . .'[69] He wrote his book because he has seen how devastating the effect of globalisation can be on 'developing countries' and 'the poor within those countries . . .'[70]

He defines globalisation as 'the removal of barriers to full trade and the closer integration of national economics . . .' This has a force for good and 'it has the *potential* to enrich everyone in the world, particularly the poor'.[71]

But globalisation needs to be radically rethought, taken away from ideology and mere politics: because during his period in office decisions were taken on the basis of ideology and politics rather than economics 'As a result many wrong-headed actions were taken, ones that did not solve the problem at hand but that fit with the interests of beliefs of the people in

---

67. Naomi Klein, *Fences and Windows: Dispatches from the Front-Lines of the Globalization Debate* (London: Flamingo, 2002), 11 speaks of attending the protest against the World Bank and the International Monetary Fund at Washington DC in April 2000 and that '[M]ost notably, former World Bank chief economist Joseph Stiglitz said the IMF was in desperate need of a large dose of democracy and transparency'. This was amid the 'rush among former World Bank and IMF officials to come out on the side of the critics and renounce their former employers'.

68. Joseph E Stiglitz, *Globalization and its Discontents* (Camberwell, Victoria: Allen Lane, 2002). Also see Joseph E Stiglitz, 'Globalization and Development', in David Held and Mathias Koenig-Archibugi (editors), *Taming Globalization: Frontiers of Governance* (Cambridge: Polity, 2003).

69. *Ibid*, xvi.

70. *Ibid*, ix.

71. *Ibid*, ix.

power'.[72] Politicisation occurred: 'academics . . . became polarized and started to bend the evidence to fit the ideas of those in charge'.[73] What he saw in Kenya, as only one example, 'showed that good economic policies have the power to change the lives of these poor people'.[74] He is a strong critic of the International Monetary Fund in the way it handles debt and bankruptcy. 'The IMF is a political institution.'[75] The IMF's policies, in part, are 'based on the outworn presumption that markets, by themselves, lead to efficient outcomes'.[76]

> The backlash against globalization draws its force not only from the perceived damage done to developing countries by policies driven by ideology but also from the inequities in the global trading system . . . forcing them (poor countries) to open up their markets to the good of the advanced industrial countries while keeping their own markets protected, policies that make the rich richer and the poor more impoverished—and increasingly angry.[77]

Stiglitz recognises the value of globalisation for the world and is acutely aware of what may go wrong, and alerts us both to that wrong and how it may be fixed. There is nothing new about protests concerning economic matters around the world, the difference is that they are also now in the developed countries.[78]

Stiglitz takes up a theme we will dwell on in this last part of the book: 'Unfortunately, we have no world government, accountable to the people of every country, to oversee the

---

72. *Ibid*, 10.
73. *Ibid*, x.
74. *Ibid*, xi.
75. *Ibid*, 166.
76. *Ibid*, xii.
77. *Ibid*, 15.
78. *Ibid*, 3.

globalization process in a fashion comparable to the way national governments guided the nationalization process'.[79]

At the close of chapter one here is Stiglitz's great hope:

> Globalization can be reshaped, and when it is, when it is properly, fairly run, with all countries having a share in policies affecting them, there is a possibility that it will help create a new global economy in which growth is not only more sustainable and less volatile but the fruits of this growth are more equitably shared.[80]

Reflecting on economics as a science Stiglitz writes that 'one of the important distinctions between *ideology* and *science* is that science recognizes the limitations on what one knows'.[81]

Stiglitz turns to development: '[S]uccessful development pays careful attention to social stability . . .'[82]

It is not just a matter of resources and capital but the 'transformation' of society. 'Development is about transforming societies, improving the lives of the poor, enabling everyone to have a chance of success and access to healthcare and education'.[83]

While addressing development, matters of culture and the religions of the people are not addressed. Stiglitz has no conception of evil in the world; he has an unshakable belief that his style of globalisation can be the best of all possible worlds.

V

In this second to last section, I would like to explore a little further the intellectual opposition to globalisation. John Gray is the professor of European thought at the London School of Economics. He writes:

---

79.   *Ibid*, 21
80.   *Ibid*, 22
81.   *Ibid*, 230
82.   *Ibid*, 77
83.   *Ibid*, 252

Globalisation begets deglobalisation . . . Neo-
liberal utopians expected that globalisation
would fill the world with liberal republics, linked
together in peace and trade. History is respon-
ding with a flowering of war, tyranny and
empire.[84]

The Australian Mark T Berger provides a Marxist view of
globalisation and he fore-grounds his unity with the anti-
globalisation movement. He believes that the US is the single
hegemonic power driving the global economy. But his book is
only a 'broad brush argument'.[85]

William T. Kavanaugh [86] has written that the

contemporary manifestation of the absorption of
civil society is the symbiosis of the state and the
corporation that signals the collapse of separation
between politics and economics . . . The greatest
distinction between one government and another
is the degree to which market replaces government or government replaces market. We live
under the former type . . . [87]

Globalisation, for Kavanaugh, is, in part, the hyperextension of
the triumph of the universal over the local on which the nation-
state is founded.[88]

---

84. John Gray, *AL QAEDA and What it Means to be Modern* (London:
     Faber and Faber, 2003), 112–3. In *False dawn: the Delusions of Global
     Capitalism* (London: Granta Books, 1998), 2002, John Gray says that
     global capitalism is falling apart.
85. Mark T Berger, *The Battle for Asia: From Decolonisation to
     Globalisation* (London: RoutledgeCurzon, 2004). Reviewed in the
     Australian Book Review by Malcom Cook, no 263, August 2004: 36–7.
86. William T Kavanaugh, 'Killing for the Telephone Company: Why the
     Nation-state is not the Keeper of the Common Good', *Modern Theology*
     20 (April 2004): 243–274.
87. *Ibid*, 258.
88. *Ibid*, 264.

The late Pope John Paul II was a constant critic of globalisation for two decades. In his 1981 encyclical *Laborem Excercens* he spoke of the need for the voice of the poor to have a role in international decision-making, even if it means a reduction or less rapid increase of material well-being for the developed nations. All people must benefit equally from globalisation. The Pope was a leader in the campaign for international debt relief. But Ira Rifkin asks, is the Vatican anti-globalisation or alter-globalisation? And, after all, the Vatican's world-wide influence 'is it a direct result of globalisation's foundational antecedents?'[89]

VI

Christian feminist and Lutheran theologian Cynthia Moe-Lobeda has written a fundamental critique of globalisation in *Healing a Broken World: Globalisation and God.*[90] I largely agree with her criticism of globalisation in the first three chapters, although I do not think she has a sufficiently developed sense and notion of 'the globe'. Chapter 6 is largely a well-told narrative of a prosperous church in North-west America which slowly but surely not only became aware of the evils of globalisation, but painfully took steps to do a little, amid their felt limitations, place and resources, to combat globalisation. The methodological appendix to the book is very dense and almost unreadable.

Chapters 4 and 5 contains her solution, and draws on the work of German theologian Martin Luther. She situates the loving immanent God of Luther immanently in human affairs, that is sacramentally embedded in the immanent life of people as they are in turn embedded in culture and creation. Moe-Lobeda's proposition has a distinctly ecological thrust. This immanence is the immanence and embeddedness of Luther's indwelling Christ of love sacramentally. This is not directly

---

89.   Ira Rifkin, 'Faithfully considering Glocalisation' *Sightings* 6/12/03. http://marty-center.uchigago.edu/ Martin Marty Centre at the University of Chicago Divinity School.

90.   Cynthia D Moe-Lobeda, *Healing a Broken World: Globalisation and God* (Minneapolitis: Fortress 2002).

applied ethically to globalisation where, rather, Moe-Lobeda employs Christian feminist and other liberationist ethics.

What has happened to Luther's transcendent God, particularly in the theological treatise he loved best, *The Bondage of the Will* (1525), against Erasmus where he comes close at times to determinism? Nor is there any mention of the Trinity. Only a transcendent God can rule and move the world and only a transcendent God can move globalisation. In our survey of globalisation God has been barely mentioned by the sources and the transcendent God not at all. Perhaps globalisation has come into being post-enlightenment as the transcendent God has been phased out of the Anglo-European tradition.

God is at one and the same time the transcendent beyond the most transcendent and the immanent nearer than the most immanent.[91]

Moe-Lobeda does not mention Luther's theology of the cross (Heidelberg Disputation, 1518). The *theologia crucis* (theology of the cross) was opposed by Luther to the *theologia gloriae* (theology of glory). He saw a 'theology of glory' in the triumphalism, hubris and arrogance of the late-mediaeval Roman Catholic Church. There is a 'theology' of glory today, I suggest, with globalisation and its proponents. It needs the antidote of the theology of the cross in which, Luther held in utter humility that Christ suffers with us and we with him in our pain. The pain of the theology of the cross can empathise with the victims of globalisation and they with it. The 'word of the cross' (1 Cor 2:2) should be triumphant. The transcendent God and the theology of the cross are a two-pronged attack on globalisation.

Then there is the ethical outcome in Luther's work which I will spell out in a three-fold way.

1. There is the doctrine of the two kingdoms (not mentioned by Moe-Lobeda) in which one kingdom is the church of believers and the other, the kingdom of Satan, is the rest of the world. Luther came later in life to modify his dualism in the doctrine by the notion of 'civil righteousness'. However, it is clear that in the doctrine

---

91.   I owe this expression to Alistair Macrae.

of the two kingdoms we have an understanding of the kingdom of God active in the world.

2. The Finnish school majors on Luther's notion of love (Heidelberg Disputation 1518) in which through justification by faith the Christian is enabled by Christ to be Christ in love to his/her brother or sister and this is a dynamic which goes on and out wider and further and further throughout the world.

3. As Lazareth shows, Luther's theological and social ethics are found through and through in his exegesis and interpretation of scripture which covers the whole of the life in the world and, given the necessary changes over 500 years, applies to our world today. These ethics apply to globalisation.[92]

92.	On Luther's transcendent God:

'Nothing would be said of God, if the whole of Christian doctrine and men also were not already involved. But the reason for this is that what is at issue in Christian doctrine and also in human existence is nothing other but the basic assertion of the existence of God . . . one must exclude everything that prevents God from being God, and which gives an opportunity of speaking of theological matters in an untheological or pseudotheological way' (246). 'Surely it is the fundamental definition of the nature of God that nothing preceded him, that nothing imposes any conditions on him, that he alone is the origin of things, and that, as it is expressed by the technical term "aseity" he derives his being from himself.' Gerhard Ebeling, *Luther: An Introduction to His Thought* (Philadelphia: Fortress, 1970), 252.

An older work is Philip S Watson, *Let God be God: an interpretation of the thought of Martin Luther* (Philadelphia: Fortress, 1966 [1947]), 15–25, 33–8. Watson likened the change of perception which Copernicus held that the earth revolved around its centre the sun and not vice versa, to Luther's displacing humans from the centre of things by *the* centre, the transcendent God.

Luther and Erasmus: Free Will and Salvation Library of Christian Classics, vol XVII, edited by E Gordon Rupp and Philip S Watson, (Philadelphia: Westminster Press, 1969).

See Mark Wriedt, 'Luther's Theology' in *The Cambridge Companion to Martin Luther*, edited by Donald K McKim (Cambridge: Cambridge University Press, 2003), 86–119.

On Luther's theology of the cross:

VII

In his last days British theologian Lesslie Newbigin, the great missionary statesman of the twentieth century, vehemently attacked the free market system and was prescient:

It has been a constant theme of my speaking and writing that the world dominance of the idolatry of the free market will, if not reversed, both

---

Luther writes: 'Truly, this wisdom of the cross and this new meaning of things is not merely unheard of, but is by far the most fearful thing even for the rulers of the church. Yet it is no wonder, since they have abandoned the Holy Scripture and have begun to read unholy writings of men and the dissertations on finances instead.' (22–3). Walther von Loewenich, *Luther's Theology of the Cross* (Minneapolis: Augsburg, 1976).

Also see Alister E McGrath, *Luther's Theology of the Cross* (Oxford: Blackwell, 1985).

On Luther's theological and social ethics:

Luther, Selected Political Writings, edited and with an introduction by JM Porter (Philadelphia: Fortress, 1974), 1–22, at 22. On Porter see Rowan Gill review in *Andover Newton Quarterly*, vol 15, no 4, March 1975: 278.

Veli-Matti Kärkkäinen, '"The Christian as Christ to the Neighbour": On Luther's Theology of Love', *International Journal of Systematic Theology* 6 (April 2004): 101–117.

William H Lazareth, *Christians in Society: Luther, the Bible and Social Ethics* (Minneapolis: Fortress 2001).

Bernd Wannenwetsch, 'Luther's Moral Theology', in *The Cambridge Companion to Martin Luther*, edited by Donald K McKim (Cambridge: Cambridge University Press, 2003), 120–135.

See also: Timothy J Wengert (editor) *Harvesting Martin Luther's Reflections on Theology, Ethics and the Church* (Grand Rapids: Eerdmans, 2004); Paul Althaus, *The Ethics of Martin Luther* (Philadelphia: Fortress, 1972).

With 500 years of interpretation, dispute and the passage of time it is hard to know the real Luther. Lazareth tackles this in his first chapter. David C Steinmetz, 'The Catholic Luther: a critical appraisal', in *Theology Today* 61 (July 2004): 187–201, is also well aware of it and seeks to pull off the layers and give us the historical Luther and his teachings.

disintegrate human society and destroy the environment . . . The ideology of the free market rests upon a doctrine of human nature that is directly attacked by the Christian faith. Idolatry cannot be countered merely by moral protest against its effects. It has to be tackled at its source . . . We have to find ways of making known the fact that the incarnate crucified and risen Christ is Lord also of the economic order.[93]

Wainwright summarises:

In fact, the ideology and practice of the free market—driven by the covetousness which the Apostle Paul called idolatry—will be Newbigin's forecast in his final years to become, with Islam, one of the two great global rivals to the Christian faith in the 21st century.[94]

Greed is called idolatry in Ephesians 5:5, Colossians 3:5 and 1 Timothy 6:10. 'Luther considered early capitalism to constitute a *status confessionis* for the church'.[95]

Hear the words of the late Davis McCaughey, an Irish born Australian theologian, which he has said with justification, and which I fully endorse and summarise my own views very adequately:

My final point is this: men and women are called by God, are redeemed by Christ into responsible

---

93. Leslie Newbigin, cited in Geoffrey Wainwrigth, *Leslie Newbegin: A Theological Life* (Oxford: Oxford University Press, 2000), 132, 207.

94. The above in Geoffrey Wainwright, *Lesslie Newbigin: A Theological Life* (Oxford: Oxford University Press, 2000), 261. Also see Rowan Gill, 'The Trinity, Western Decadence and Islam', in *Zadok Perspectives* 82, Autumn 2004: 16–17.

95. Carter Lindberg, 'Luther's Struggle with Social-Ethical Issues', in *The Cambridge Companion to Martin Luther*, edited by Donald K McKim (Cambridge: Cambridge University Press, 2003), 165–178, at 173.

relationships. As far as I know, God did not say at the beginning 'Let us create market forces to look after the wellbeing of my creatures'. He said 'Let us make man (ie human beings) in our image' with responsibilities in and for the created world. So God created in his own image, male and female created he them. Similarly I am not aware that the new man and woman in Christ have been redeemed to a state of passivity, to await the succeeding of recession with recovery, the turning of the wheel of the trade cycle. He and she have been redeemed to love neighbour as self, and that means making sacrifices and taking responsibilities . . . At a more reflective level the word 'value' or 'values', and even the word 'virtue' has come back into our vocabulary. There are some people brave enough to suggest that that impersonal force, the market, in which we are supposed to believe with superstitious awe as controlling our destiny, may be manipulated or controlled by human beings actually making judgments on behalf of other human beings. Maybe the market is not value-free. Maybe somebody actually decides what shall be fed into the computer! Insofar as that decision is good or bad it is a moral decision.[96]

By way of conclusion I turn to feminist theologian Sallie McFague and her book *Life Abundant*.[97] She models Christian, and thus human life, after the shape and form of economy, and

---

96. Davis McCaughey in *Fresh Words and Deeds: The McCaughey Papers* edited by Peter Matheson and Christiaan Mostert (Melbourne, David Lovell Publishing, 2004), 34, 37. See Also M Douglas Meeks, *God the Economist: The Doctrine of God and Political Economy* (Minneapolis: Fortress Press, 1989).

97. Sallie McFague, *Life Abundant: Rethinking Theology and Economy for a Planet in Peril* (Minneapolis: Fortress Press, 2001), chapters 4 and 5 and then *passim*.

'ecological economic paradigm' to be precise, which is opposed to the 'Neo-classical economic paradigm' with which she also models.

She opposes its commodification, its consumer society, its individualism and the isolation of the economy from the planet's well-being. Its anthropology is self-contradictory. 'Economics is a discipline, a field of study, to help people attain their goals; it is not, or should not be, the ideology that sets those goals' (95).

Her model is filled out in terms of the household and ecology (both words come from the Greek *oikonomia* which gives us 'economy', 'ecumenical' and *homo econimicus*). This paradigm is very close to the earth and loving planet earth which is God's body. This is her power and her weakness: she's able to undercut many criticism of ecology and on the other hand stress a great ecological love. Whether the earth as God's body is orthodox is another question.[98]

McFague has two notions of globalisation: 'Globalisation is not the opening of markets to free trade so that six people who possess fifty-nine per cent of the world's wealth can get even more. Globalisation in the ecological model means a decent life on a sustainable planet for all human beings'.[99] Her refrain throughout the book is Irenaeus's third century saying: The glory of God is every creature fully alive. She sees herself at the cutting edge of an ecological revolution (210).

The great strength of McFague's mature work—'in opposition to the neo-classical world view of regnant economics'—is her notion of the earth as the body of God which in giving her an extremely immanentist view enables her to affirm all people, creatures and earth directly in their being but makes her depart from the norm in Christology which may be heterodox.

---

98. See *The Body of God: An Ecological Theology* (Minneapolis: Fortress Press, 1993) and *Models of God: Theology for an Ecological, Nuclear Age* (Minneapolis: Fortress Press, 1987).

99. *Life Abundant*, 122.

American Empire

Globalisation is coterminous with America or Americanisation. Friedman thought so for he wrote: 'Globalisation is American-isation'.[1] Other voices have been raised agreeing with this view. Haroun Er-Rashid, Professor in the School of Environmental Sciences and Management of the Independent University of Bangladesh: 'With globalisation the economic power of the United States may reach such proportions that in many countries nothing may be left of local economies'.[2]

AS Gammal writes:

> Globalisation is essentially an economic process that begins in America and eventually involves its trilateral partners in Europe and Japan. Taking the ideology of neo-liberalism as its rhetorical fuel, globalisation seeks to create a world economy that benefits American corporations, first and foremost, and other trans-national companies that operate by American-defined rules.[3]

Zafar Bangash writes:

> Globalisation means not merely uniformity but also conformity to the dominant, primarily American, culture. This applies as much to food as it does to music and clothes. People around the world are expected to eat greasy McDonalds'

1. Friedman, *The Lexus and the Olive Tree*, 294. See also 293, 340, 344, 357, 383, 392, 395, 396, 405, 433 and 437.
2. Haroun Er-Rashid, 'Muslims and the West: A Paradox of Polarisation', in *Islam and the West: Critical Perspectives on Modernity*, edited by Michael J Thompson (Lanham Boulder New York and Oxford: Rowman and Littlefield Publishers Inc, 2003), 7.
3. AS Gammal, 'The Global Protests against Globalisation and the Media's Coverage of them', *Crescent International*, June 1–15, 2001.

hamburgers, drink pepsi or coke, wear levi jeans
and gyrate to Michael Jackson music. If they have
any spare time left, then the ubiquitous CNN is
there to occupy it.[4]

When Jessica Stein asked Abu Shanab, a member of Hamas,
in the American summer of 1999, what he thought of
globalisation, he said: 'Globalisation is just a new colonial
system. It is America's attempt to dominate the rest of the
world economically rather than militarily.'[5]

I

Central to the notion of American imperialism is the idea of
'Manifest Destiny'. The idea was originated by John L
O'Sullivan in his political magazine *Democratic Review* in the
1830s and 1840s:

> [America has] the right of our manifest destiny to
> overspread and possess the whole of the
> continent which Providence has given us for the
> development of the great experiment of liberty
> and federaltive [sic] development of self
> government entrusted to us. It is the right such as
> that of the tree to space of air and the earth
> suitable for the full expansion of its principle and
> destiny of growth.[6]

---

4.   Zafar Bangas, 'McDonaldization of Culture: America's pervasive
      influence globally', *Crescent International*, February 1–15, 1998. The
      last two quotations are found in Peter G Riddell and Peter Cotterell
      Islam in Context: Past, Present and Future (Grand Rapids: Baker
      Academic, 2003), 158.

5.   Jessica Stein, *Terror in the Name of God: Why Religious Militants Kill*
      (New York: Ecco (an imprint of HarperCollins), 2003), 40. Jessica
      Stein is an American-Jewish academic who had easy access to
      Christian, Jewish and Muslim terrorists.

6.   John L O'Sullivan, 'Annexation', *United States Magazine and
      Democratic Review*, July–August 1845, vol 17, Issue 085-086: 5–10.
      Cornell University holds these materials in its archives.

So 'Manifest Destiny' was originally a doctrine which legitimised the subjugation of the American continent for the American people over the Native Americans and the ecology from the thirteen states of the eastern seaboard through the various frontiers and on to the Western coast after war with Mexico. This originally involved a certain amount of isolationism from the rest of the world.[7]

> It is clear that in the [1890s] the spirit of 'manifest destiny', long dormant, was once more abroad in the land. The precise manifestations of that destiny differed, but the ideology was fundamentally the same as that which had animated an earlier generation. The phrase had once served as a rationalisation for the conquest of Texas and California; it was now to serve as a rationalisation for a 'large policy' in the Caribbean, the Pacific and the Far East. Now that the continent was conquered, it was the ineluctable destiny of the United States to become a world power . . . The Republican platform of 1892 called for 'the achievement of the manifest destiny of the Republic in its broadest sense'. When after a decade of tumult and shouting the noise died down, the United States found herself in fact a world power, owning the extra territorial lands of Puerto Rico, Hawaii, Wake, Guam,

---

7.   Samuel Eliot Morison and Henry Steele Commager, *The Growth of the American Republic*, vol 1 (New York: Oxford University Press, 1962), 315, 605–8, 616, 633. 'Nine years later [1845] President James K Polk, a fervent expansionist, proclaimed that the country should fill its natural boundaries and reach its 'manifest destiny' . . . [regarding the American Civil War] . . . a religious crisis raged over whether the country's manifest destiny was of a slave or a free nature . . . Religion has always found fertile soil in the United States, from Native American shamanism to Euro-American myths of providential foundings in a new Eden and manifest destinies to subdue the earth.' In Russell Duncan and Joseph Goddard, *Contemporary America* (New York: Palgrave, 2003), 13, 16, 152.

Tutuila and the Philippines, exercising protec-
torates over Cuba, Panama and Nicaragua and
asserting its interest and influence in the far east.[8]

O'Sullivan continues:

> [O]ur national birth was the beginning of a new
> history, the formation and progress of an untried
> political system, which separates us from the past
> and connects us with the future only, and so far
> as regards the entire development of the natural
> rights of man, in moral, political and national life,
> we may confidently assume that our country is
> destined to be the great nation of futurity . . . We
> are the nation of human progress, and who will,
> what can, set limits to our onward march?
> Providence is with us, and no earthly power can .
> . . For this blessed mission to the nations of the
> world, which are shut out from the life-giving
> light of the truth, has America been chosen; and
> her high example shall smite unto death the
> tyranny of kings, hierarchs, and oligarchs, and
> carry the glad tidings of peace and goodwill
> where myriads now endure existence scarcely
> more enviable than that of beasts of the field.
> Who then can doubt that our country is destined
> to be the great nation of futurity.[9]

That is why James A Marone can call the thirteenth chapter
of his book *Manifest Destiny and the Cold War*.[10]

Missiologist, David J Bosch, of blessed memory, traces
'Manifest Destiny' back to the spirit of the Enlightenment and

---

8.   Samuel Eliot Morison and Henry Steele Commager, *The Growth of the American Republic*, vol 2 (New York: Oxford University Press, 1962), 414. Also see 415 ff.

9.   John L O'Sullivan, 'The Great Nation of Futurity', *United States Magazine and Democratic Review*, November 1839, Issue 23, 426–430.

10. James A Marone, *Hellfire Nation: the Politics of Sin in American History* (New Haven and London: Yale University Press, 2003), 378–406.

the egalitarianism it inspired in the West with the toppling of crowned heads and hierarchical governments from the French Revolution onward. 'Manifest Destiny' was a product of nationalism and that most of all in the United States which had no ghosts from the past to cloud its visions. Indeed the notion of 'Manifest Destiny' was first of all a puritan idea and force which had more play in the United States—an almost unfettered passage—than it did in England where puritanism lasted but a short time. So, it arose much earlier in the United States than elsewhere and was Anglo-Saxon and the Anglo-Saxon race shaking off the British yoke in 1776 allowed the Americans to vent more freely their ideas of 'Manifest Destiny'. With the advent of post-millenialism the hope arose that a church missionary movement would Christianise the whole world before the second Advent. Thus 'Manifest Destiny' was transmuted into the worldwide missionary movement as it emanated from the United States. Was the motivation nationalist or religious? The foreign missionary enterprise involved thousands of Americans abroad and millions at home during the 1880s and 1890s. Missionary enthusiasm was at its peak at the New York Ecumenical Conference of 1900 which was the 'largest missionary conference ever held' with 200 missionary societies participating, nearly 200,000 people attending, and Presidents Harrison and McKinley and Governor Theodore Roosevelt of New York giving the lead! They felt a 'debt' to those living in darkness overseas, a debt which turned into 'the white man's burden'. Bosch summarises by sheeting home the forces of 'Manifest Destiny' to the spirit of the Enlightenment.[11]

'Captain America' is a comic book character who, however, comes from the darkest and most zealous side of America's history of civil religion. He is completely white and right, God is utterly on his side, and he must obliterate the enemies of God. His ideology is completely a mirror image of that of the Muslim

---

11.   Daniel J Bosch, *Transforming Mission: Paradigm Shifts in Theology of Mission* (New York: Orbis, 1994 [1991]), 298–302, 310, 332. I owe the quotations from O'Sullivan above to Ziauddin Sardar and Merryl Wyn Davies *Why do People Hate America?* (Cambridge: Icon, 2002).

fundamentalists and vice versa. This ideology of 'Captain America' informs much of America's contemporary religious right.[12]

American imperialism was a Protestant force as is seen in Martin Marty's bicentennial history *Righteous Empire*.[13]

This is seen in the power invested in America's twentieth century presidents, especially since Franklin Delano Roosevelt.[14]

Hollywood is a powerful force in America's attempted imperialism over the world.[15]

II

According to President George Walker Bush: 'America has no empire to extend or utopia to establish. We wish for others what we wish for ourselves—safety from violence, the rewards of liberty and the hope for a better life'(Graduation speech at West Point, 1 June 2002).[16]

President Bush has also said: 'America has never been an empire. It may be the only great power in history that had the

---

12.   Robert Jewett and John Shelton Lawrence, *Captain America and the Crusade against Evil: The Dilemma of Zealous Nationalism* (Grand Rapids: Eerdman, 2003).

13.   Martin E Marty, *Righteous Empire: The Protestant Experience in America* (New York: The Dial Press, 1970). Also see Sydney E Ahlstrom, *The Religious History of the American People* (New Haven: Yale University Press, 1972).

14.   Richard E Neustadt, *Presidential Power and the Modern Presidents: The Politics of Leadership from Roosevelt to Reagan* (New York: The Free Press, 1990); Martin Walker, 'Teddy Roosevelt and the American Ambition' in *Makers of the American Century* (London: Vintage, 2001), 3–16; Martin Walker, 'Franklin D Roosevelt and the American Solution' in *Makers of the American Century*, 160–175; Sidney Blumenthal, *The Clinton Wars: an insider's account of the White House Years* (Camberwell, Victoria: Viking (an imprint of Penguin Books) 2003); Peter Singer, *The President of Good and Evil: The Ethics of George W Bush* (Melbourne: Text, 2004).

15.   Ella Shoht and Robert Stam, 'The Imperial Imaginary' in *The Film Cultures Reader*, edited by Graeme Turner (London and New York: Routledge, 2002), 366–378.

16.   Quoted by Peter Singer, *The President of Good and Evil: the Ethics of George W Bush* (Melbourne: Text, 2004), 232.

chance, and refused—preferring greatness to power and justice to glory.'[17]

From now on in this section I will deal with the ramifications of the contemporary American empire. The two above quotations from President Bush are evidence, I suggest, of being monumentally in denial.

Niall Ferguson is the Herzog Professor of Financial History at the Stern School of Business, New York University. He is also a Senior Research Fellow of Jesus College at Oxford and a Senior Fellow of the Hoover Institution, Stanford University. He is the acclaimed author of a study on the British Empire. Now comes *Colossus: The Rise and Fall of the American Empire*.[18]

Ferguson argues that not only is the US an empire, but it has always been an empire. We require a liberal empire, although the US has been a surprisingly inept empire builder. Thomas Jefferson had spoken of an 'empire of liberty' (2).

In November 2000, Richard Haass, who became the Bush administration's director of policy planning clearly called for an 'informal American empire'. A month after 9/11 Max Boot made out the 'case for an American empire' (4). In 2002 the journalist Sebastian Mallaby proposed American 'neo-imperialism'. The majority of the new imperialists were neo-conservatives (5).

The US is an empire in denial. Colin Powell, former Secretary of State, has said: 'The United States does not seek a territorial empire. We have never been imperialists. We seek a world in which liberty, prosperity and peace can become the heritage of all peoples and not just the exclusive privilege of the few.'

---

17.   Quoted in Andrew J Bacevich, *American Empire: the Realities and Consequences of US Diplomacy* (Cambridge, Mass. and London: 2002), 201.

18.   Niall Ferguson, *Colossus: The Rise and Fall of the American Empire* (London: Allen Lane [an imprint of Penguin Books], 2004). For a review of the book see Michael Gawenda, editor-in-chief of *The Age*, 4 September 2004. All references to Ferguson's book are in the body of our text.

After 9/11 it was expected, and happened, that Americans would deny their imperialism more than ever while foreign policy was moving from the defence to the offence (7).

The US is a 'hegemony', a term first used when the Greek city states formed the league against the Roman Empire (8–9). A hegemon can be more powerful than an empire (10). The American phenomenon has most usually been compared with the Roman Empire (12).

Ferguson is in favour of there being an empire like America's at the present time. Here is how he sums up the American empire:

> It goes without saying that it is a liberal democracy and market economy, though its polity has some illiberal characteristics and its economy a high level of state intervention ('mixed' might be more accurate than 'market'). It is primarily concerned with its own security and maintaining international communications and, secondarily, with ensuring access to raw materials (principally, though not exclusively, oil). It is also in the business of providing a limited number of public goods: peace, by intervening against some bellicose regimes and in some civil wars; freedom of the seas and skies for trade; and a distinctive form of 'conversion' usually called Americanisation, which is carried out . . . by the exporters of American consumer goods and as entertainment. Its methods of formal rule are primarily military in character; the methods of informal rule rely heavily on non-governmental organisations and corporations and in some cases local elites (13).

The greatest shortcoming of American imperialism is, what Ferguson calls 'its excessively short-term horizon', that is a very limited follow-through on imperialistic activity overseas (13). Paradoxically, therefore, the US has engaged in some important items of follow-through, eg Japan, South Korea and West Germany since 1945. American bases, also, are proliferating the globe. The Pentagon's military budget is equal to the budgets of the next twelve to fifteen nations combined (16).

In the Cold War the Soviet Union 'overstretched' first and as an introductory remark Ferguson is prepared to say that 'there seems little danger of imminent imperial overstretch' in the US (17–19).

Ferguson points to the 'multinationals' 'a substantial number of which . . . are American in origin and continue to have their headquarters in the United States' (18). He refers, for example, to McDonalds, Coca Cola, Microsoft and Time Warner. McDonalds has spread all over the world with great strength and with great representation in other countries but is still decidedly American.

'Soft power' =Americanisation and is indirect, intuitive, culture influence which the empire still uses (20). 'Soft power is merely the velvet glove concealing an iron hand' (24).[19]

Ferguson clarifies what he means by liberal empire: '[A]ll empires are exploitative in character. Yet there can be . . . such a thing as a liberal empire, one that enhances its own security and prosperity precisely by providing the rest of the world with generally beneficial public goods: not only economic freedom but also the institutions necessary for markets to flourish' (24–25). Obviously this is his ideal.[20]

In the first chapter Ferguson traces the history of the American empire until the Great War. He cites a disagreement between the British and Woodrow Wilson and says: 'Thus was born the paradox that was to be a characteristic feature of American foreign policy for a century: the paradox of dictating democracy, of enforcing freedom, of extorting emancipation' (54).

---

19. This is what Michael Ignatieff means when he addresses the 'flip-flop' of American imperialism as, in his terms, 'Empire Lite': Michael Ignatieff, *Empire Lite: Nation-Building in Bosnia, Kosova and Afghanistan* (London: Vintage, 2003).

20. Ellen T Charry 'Virtual Salvation' *Theology Today* 61 (October 2004) 334–346, especially at 335, is a firm supporter of the American view. Jean Bethke Elshtain, who was thought to be left of centre, is a quite prominent American theologian who supported the Iraq war.

Ferguson's second chapter traces the great difficulty America had in its many interventions around the world in the twentieth century and explains the success stories of West Germany, Japan and South Korea. The reason: it was an empire in denial (63) and 'imperialism of anti-imperialism' (78). 'America should fight only when its national interests are at stake; imperiled regimes looking for US sponsorship would henceforth have to do the dirty work themselves' (101).

Amid this there is Truman's forthright statement: 'The only way to 'save the world from totalitarianism . . . was for the whole world [to] adopt the American system "for" the American system' could survive only by becoming the world system' (80). Regarding the success stories, Ferguson says of West Germany: 'This was not so much an empire by invitation as an empire by improvisation' (75).

The third chapter discusses September 11, 2001 as the definitive definition of a lot of trends in the United States, but Ferguson claims that November 9, 1989, the fall of the Berlin Wall, was more important and was the real beginning of the twenty-first century.

With chapter 4, Ferguson puts forward the argument that the United States in Iraq descended from multi-lateralism to uni-lateralism since 1990 and that the United Nations had difficulty finding a consistent policy.

> It was during the 1990s that the United States learned, through bitter experience, the value of credible military interventions in countries where state terror was being used against ethnic minorities. It also learned that these did not require explicit authorisation in the form of United Nations Security Council resolutions. 'Coalitions of the willing' could suffice (27).

I flatly oppose this on the basis of international law.

In chapter 5 the case is made for a liberal empire post-Afghanistan and Iraq, 'the last great Anglophone empire' (27). He makes an altruistic argument for this (198). The problem with this is that Iraq is not yet a completed situation but, like the Israeli situation, is looking more and more like Vietnam all over again.

In chapter 6 Ferguson addresses Iraq and with a cost-benefit analysis:

> however, it is far from clear as I write that the United States is capable of committing either the manpower or the time needed to make a success of its 'nation building' in Iraq, much less in Afghanistan. This is primarily because the American electorate is averse to the kind of long-term commitment that history strongly suggests is necessary to achieve a successful transition to a market economy and representative government. Though I fervently hope to be proved wrong, I question therefore whether America has the capacity 'to build effective civilian institutions in Iraq, given its historic preference for short-term, primarily military interventions and its reluctance to learn that these seldom, if ever, work (28).

In February 2004 President George Walker Bush announced from the White House lawn that the occupying military power in Iraq would hand over sovereignty to a civilian Iraqi government on June 30, 2004. As he turned away from the lectern he added: 'and leave them with American values'. The pornographic atrocities (the word of Australian Foreign Minister Alexander Downer) of Abu Ghraib Prison revealed in May puts the lie to 'American values' and called forth rage in the Muslim world. At the G8 Summit of world leaders at Savannah, Georgia, on June 11, President Jacques Chirac of France said one could not grow a culture in a few moments.

Ferguson in his concluding chapter infers that the American empire rests on weaker foundations than might have been supposed. Americans 'lack the imperial cast of mind. They would rather consume than conquer' (29). 'Consequently, and very regrettably, it is quite conceivable that their empire could unravel as swiftly as the equally "anti-imperial" empire that was the Soviet Union' (29).[21]

If the American empire deteriorates or collapses its overstretch will occur at home. Morris Berman believes that it is occurring now for four reasons. First, increasing social and economic inequality. Since 1979 a total of forty-three million jobs have been lost. The country is taking more of a third world aspect. Second, there is an incapacity to handle adequately support programs. Third, there is a collapse of American intelligence. Basic knowledge is often unknown; infotainment is looked for more and more. Fourth, there is spiritual death. This is seen in ridiculous wacky religious life.[22]

---

21.   Ferguson is a fervent believer in globalisation and it meshes with his main thesis: 'The real problem with the early 20th century is not globalisation but its absence or inhibition. Indeed the sad truth about globalisation is that it is not truly global at all' (177). 'One reason that modern globalisation is associated with high levels of inequality is that there are so many restrictions on the free movement of labour from less developed to developed societies' (177). 'The globalisation of warfare in the 20th century must bear a large share of responsibility for the mid-century breakdown of international trade, capital flows and migration' (185). 'The paradox of globalisation is that as the world becomes more integrated, so power becomes more diffuse' (298). 'Unlike most European critics of the United States, then, I believe the world needs an effective liberal empire and the United States is the best candidate for the job. Economic globalisation is working. The rapid growth per capita incomes in the world's most populous countries, China and India, means that international inequality is finally narrowing . . . economic globalisation needs to be underwritten politically, as it was a century ago' (301).

22.   Morris Berman, *The Twilight of American Culture* (London: Norton, 2001). Also see Naomi Klein, *Fences and Windows*, 115 ff. Professor Ross Buckley is a director of the Tim Fisher Centre for Global Trade and Finance at Bond University. He writes in a similar way: 'how the fourth of July story has defined the American Spirit'. *The Age* 4 July 2005, 13. Also see Richard Florida, The Flight of the Creative Class: *The New Global Competition for Talent* (New York: HarperBusiness, 2005), as reviewed in *The Weekend Australian Review* 9/10 July 2005, page 10. Especially see Jared Diamond, Collapse: How Societies Choose to Fail or Survive (Carlton, Vic: Allen Lane, 2005), particularly chapters 1, 14, 15, and 16.

III

I turn to Australian studies of the American empire by Owen Harries, Christian Reus-Smit and Robert Manne.

Owen Harries is an international affairs expert. He has been director of policy planning for the Australian Department of Foreign Affairs, senior advisor to Prime Minister Fraser, and Australian ambassador to UNESCO. He helped found the Washington-based foreign policy periodical *The National Interest* in 1985 of which he is editor emeritus, and currently he is senior fellow at the Sydney-based Centre for Independent Studies.

Owen Harries gave the prestigious Boyer lectures in 2003.[23] Harries has superb contacts inside the American foreign policy establishment, both conservative and neo-conservative.

He argues that with the collapse of the Soviet Union America found itself, without warning, in a position of sole super-power hegemony not knowing what to do, but with a defence budget larger than all of the other major powers combined. The sheer speed with which this change occurred meant that no other power challenged such hegemony as would normally have been the case in such a situation.

A clear vision was not enunciated and it was only with September 11, 2001 that the United States gained 'the clear purpose (or) central organising principle "namely" the war on terrorism'. 'In an instant the terrorists had given the country the clear purpose, the central organising principle, that it had previously lacked, and that some had been strenuously demanding'.

Americans 'gained a profound belief that their country (was) destined to reshape the world'. This belief was put into policy in President Bush's 2002 National Security Strategy. Harries considers this document to be the most important foreign policy statement since the Truman Doctrine of 1947. America was to

---

23. Owen Harries, *Benign or Imperial? Reflections on American Hegemony. The Boyer Lectures 2003* (Melbourne: ABC Books, 2004). The lectures were also serialised in *The Age* November 14, November 21, 28 November, 5 December, 12 December, 19–20 December 2003. The book and lectures are reviewed in *Eureka Street*, vol 14 no 5 (June 2004): 42, and the *Australian Book Review* no 260 (April 2004) 13–14.

transform the globe politically. Harries asks will other powers be willing to accept that double standard inherent in the American attempt to build its own armed forces while limiting others drastically? He doubts it. 'The whole history of international politics suggests that they will not'.

Harries speaks of democracy. Will America be able to export it? He thinks not and points to America's experience in the Caribbean, Haiti and Nicaragua.

Potential challengers to the United States are China and Europe. Neither will challenge the US militarily. The real challenge will come from inside America.

Harries is opposed to the involvement of Australia in the Iraq war, the reason why this series of Boyer Lectures has become most controversial. He warns of a too easy identification of Australian and American influence. Australia's involvement has increased our chances of becoming a terrorist target. He calls Australia's move 'surprising'.

Ralph Carolan, writing in *Eureka Street*, says:

> Toward this end (the 2002 National Security Strategy), the strategy expresses a commitment to use the US military pre-emptively and, of necessity, unilaterally. Harries argues that such use of liberal democracy is a precarious business, which is seldom successful and often produces unintended consequences. Here, Harries' analysis takes on a certain urgency, as the success of the 'coalition of the willing' in Iraq becomes not just crucial for the future of Iraq, but for the future of America's newly stated ambitions. If Iraq is seen to be a test case for the strategy, then failure would mean not simply the collapse of liberal democracy in Iraq, but the collapse of US foreign policy as it currently stands. Already the parallels with Vietnam are striking.

Christian Reus-Smit is Professor and Head of the Department of International Relations in the Research School of

Pacific and Asian Studies at the Australian National University. He has written the book *American Power and World Order*.[24]

He writes of the present situation:

> I became increasingly interested in what I see as a growing disjunction between America's material resources and its ability to translate those into intended political outcomes. I found myself arguing that there is something deeply dysfunctional, even idealistic, about the understanding of power currently informing American foreign policy, and that this is already frustrating the United States' political influence (x).

He quotes the writer Kenneth N Waltz: 'Never since Rome has one country so nearly dominated the world' (1).

Reus-Smit defines a hegemon: 'A state is hegemonic when it has the capacity to define the rules of international society' (10).

Chapter 1 traces the rise to ascendancy in American politics of the neo-conservatives in the 1990s. The tidal shift occurred with the 'handing' of the 2000 election to George W Bush and September 11, 2001. Its doctrine of power and politics

> is a curious and potentially dangerous mixture of material self-confidence, universalizing self interest and unreflective faith in America's transformative capacities, one that overstates the salience of material resources, ignores the social bases of power and denies the complexities of global political life' (4–5).

Chapter 2 says that underlying the Bush doctrine of power 'is a theory of power, one that is possessive, primarily material, subjective and decidedly non-social' (5). This has three flaws: that there is a single causal relation between material power and influence, neo-conservative legitimacy rests only on

---

24.   Christian Reus-Smit, *American Power and World Order* (Cambridge, UK: Polity, 2004). All citations are in the body of the text.

national interests, and, the cultural magnetism of the United States is assumed. Given these flaws Reus-Smit goes on to outline an alternative: a social conception of power.

In chapter 3 Reus-Smit compares the world today with that of fifty years ago because the neo-conservatives assume they are the same and neo-conservatives think that America's role is the same. They are quite different. Today's consolidation of sovereign states and liberal market economies 'have produced a triad of destabilizing side-effects; the 'domestication' of war, the persistent maldistribution of global wealth and the crisis in the global eco-system' (7). These are profound challenges for American leadership.

With chapter 4 Reus-Smit examines the ethical bases of hegemony. 'I propose a pragmatic synthesis which gives normative priority to institutionally governed change' (7).

In the final chapter Reus-Smit 'brings the discussion to a close by considering the implications of the Bush Administration's dysfunctional understanding of American power for the pursuit of American interests and the future of the global order' (8). The result is an unethical foreign policy. United States is 'anti-diplomatic': hence their frustration with the world around them which leads to their breach or neglect of the peace.

Robert Manne is Professor of Politics at Latrobe University.[25] Manne outlines the quick-sands of lying surrounding the American decision to go to war against Iraq and backgrounds it by tracing the immediate history of the neo-conservatives in American government.

We simply allude to two studies of the anxieties two distinguished Americans have about the situation of their people, first the theologian, Robert W Jenson, and, second, former United Nations Weapons Inspector Scott Ritter.[26]

---

25.   Robert Manne, 'Lying in Politics: Thoughts on Iraq', *Australian Book Review*, No 264, (September 2004): 26–32.

26.   Robert W Jenson, *Systematic Theology*, vol 2 (New York: Oxford University Press, 1999), 314–7; Scott Ritter, *Frontier Justice: Weapons of Mass Destruction and the Bushwacking of America* (Melbourne: Scribe, 2003). For an expansive, critical, but nuanced view of George Bush's America, particularly Washington DC, see Patrick McCuaghey, 'Divided They Stand', in *The Sunday Age Extra*, 3 July 2005, 17. See

There is a growing dislike of America around the world as a consequence of its operations as an empire which has led to rage in the Muslim world with America's prolonged operations in Iraq and its influence in Palestine. After reading Reus-Smit's book one can readily understand why this is so.[27]

No discussion of the subject matter of this chapter would be complete without the objective and unbiased appraisal of the thought of Noam Chomsky.[28]

---

also Don Watson, 'America Enigma', in *The Age Good Weekend* 16 July 2005, 35–40.

27. Ziauddin Sardar and Merryl Wyn Davies, *Why do People Hate America,* (Cambridge, UK: Icon, 2002); Meic Pearse, *Why the Rest Hates the West* (London: SPCK, 2003)—this book has been misnamed for it is more a very astute defence of traditional morality; ABC TV program June 19 2003 'What the World Thinks of America'. *Granta* 77 2002 asked many writers living outside of America what they thought of it. No response was so dark and foreboding as that of activist and playwright Harold Pinter (66–9).

28. See the following works: *Understanding Power: The Indispensable Chomsky*, edited by Peter R Mitchel and John Schofield (Melbourne: Scribe Publications, 2002); Noam Chomsky, *Hegonomy or Survival: America's Quest for Global Dominance?* (Crows Nest, NSW: Allan and Unwin, 2003); Noam Chomsky, *Power and Terror: Post 9/11 Talks and Interviews*, edited by John Junkeman and Takei Masakazu (New York and Little More, Tokyo: Seven Stories Press, 2003); Alison Edgley, *The Social and Political Thought of Noam Chomsky* (London and New York: Routledge, 2002); Neil Smith, *Chomsky: ideas and Ideals*, second edition (Cambridge: Cambridge University Press, 2004); Robert F Barsky, *Noam Chomsky: A Life of Dissent* (Cambridge, Mass and London: MIT Press, 1997). See also Edward W Said, *Orientalism: Western Concepts of the Orient* (London: Routledge and Keegan Paul, 1978). This is a classic on Western imperialism of the East with which contemporary American imperialism ought to be compared and its genesis enumerated. The Americans have learnt nothing from Said, especially now that the Orient is fighting back. See also, Edward W Said, *Culture and Imperialism* (London: Chatto and Windus, 1993), where Said brings the situation up to the early nineties in the West and seeks to deal with it. For his last word before his death in 2003 see Edward W Said, *From Oslo to Iraq and the Roadmap* (London: Bloomsbury, 2004).

World Government

In reading the twentieth century from a position of advantage in the twenty-first, there was a great deal of optimism and hope for a world government. It was President Woodrow Wilson's aim when he propounded the League of Nations at the close of the First World War, but his hopes were thwarted mainly because his own Congress would not support it—thus keeping the United States of America out of the League of Nations—and by the events of the 1920s and 1930s, especially the period of the Depression, and the advent of fascism and communism in Europe. On the other hand, a similar hope was held out for the United Nations among its founders, when the UN was put into place at the end of World War Two. The United Nations has survived for sixty years and been a force for unity and peace in the world—that the League of Nations could never have had—and this despite the UN's faults, and it has spawned a host of international organisations like, for example, UNESCO, the International Court of Justice and now the International Criminal Court, etc which are broadly under the umbrella of world governance. In the twentieth century's quest for hope, justice, peace and violence-free international unity, the olympic games with a quasi-religious aura cannot be forgotten. Begun by Baron de Coubertain in the last decade of the nineteenth century the games ever since have been an ideal for excellence and peace and joy that cannot be overlooked.

How would a world government be structured? It would represent all nation-states, non-government organisations, regions, tribes and trans-national corporations democratically with an executive which was equally democratic and representative that had teeth.

Opinions, however, are divided on whether we need a world government.[1]

---

1. Thomas Friedman has written of 'celestial' world government with a twinkle in his eye. Joseph S Nye Jnr, *The Paradox of American Power* (Oxford: Oxford University Press, 2002), 104, does not favour world

I foresee a world government to which the religions of the world make a significant contribution, in that a dialogical inter-faith ethic would inform such a government. Professor Hans Küng, Professor of Ecumenical Theology at Tübingen in Germany has been the most creative advocate of a true inter-faith ethic, especially convening the Parliament of World's Religions at Chicago in 1993—like a similar parliament which met in Chicago in the dying embers of the nineteenth century. Küng's effort agreed on an inter-faith ethic; an ethic which was to be put in place without any one religion abandoning its own particular truth claims.[2] A sketch of the ethic of where the 1993

---

government. Nye is Dean of the Kennedy School of Government at Harvard. Australian Hugh Stretton, *Economics: A New Introduction*, (Sydney: UNSW Press, 2000), 840–2, canvasses the subject fully and seems to be fully open to it. Michael Ignatieff, *The Lesser Evil: Political Ethics in an Age of Terror* (Edinburgh: Edinburgh University Press, 2004), 156, 167, 165 also seems open to it; Peter Singer, The *President of Good and Evil: The Ethics of George W Bush* (Text, Melbourne, 2004), 220–1, 226, 228–9, 232, 235 does too, and his particular discussion of Hobbes regarding governance illuminates this part of my book. Friedman and Stiglitz have made pertinent remarks about world governance in this book.

2.   The Declaration at the Parliament comes in two forms in English:
Hans Küng and Karl-Josef Kuschel, editors, *A Global Ethic: The Declaration of the Parliament of the World's Religions* (London: SCM, 1993), and Hans Küng and Helmut Schmidt, editors, *A Global Ethic and Global Responsibilities: Two Declarations* (London: SCM, 1993, 1998). Küng originally published *Christianity and the World Relgions*, being a dialogue with Islam, Hinduism and Buddhism (New York: Doubleday, 1986). He published an equally large book with Julia Ching, *Christianity and Chinese Religions* (New York: Doubleday, 1989). The turning point came with a small book *Global Responsibility: In Search of a New World Ethic* (London: SCM, 1990), when he launched himself fully into the project, first to publish a planned three volume inter-locking set on the 'Religions of the Book'. Two massive tomes appeared, Judaism in 1992 and Christianity in 1995. The companion volume on Islam has not yet appeared. See also Hans Küng, *Tracing the Way: Spiritual Dimensions of the World Religions* (London: Continuum, 2002). On these themes see *Eureka Street*, vol 15, no 1, January–February 2005 pages 9, 12–13, 16–17.

conference came to is as follows: Commitment to a culture of non-violence and respect for life; commitment to a culture of solidarity and a just economic order; commitment to a culture of tolerance and a life of truthfulness; commitment to a culture of equal rights and partnership between men and women. The final point was that there should be 'a transformation of consciousness'. In terms of Christianity it could mean coming to faith, growing in faith or conversion.

If such an ethic informs world government, then we would have a world situation analogous to and similar to the Constantinian settlement in Christianity in the fourth century.

Imagine the executive of a world government imposing sanctions on the United States!

If his Gifford Lectures on political ethics are anything to go by, Professor Michael Ignatieff, Carr Professor and Director of the Carr Centre for Human Rights Policy at the Kennedy School of Government, Harvard University, could well contribute to a world ethic. Hans Küng already has with *A Global Ethic for Global Politics and Economics*.[3]

World government would be *for* justice for the peoples of the world, banishing inequities; the advent of peace, hope, justice, love, joy and adequate communications for all; from Boston to Bangladesh and back, from Tokyo to Tikrit and back, from Melbourne to Moscow and back et al.

We are one world[4]—Marshall McLuhan's global village —and unity is close to our possession. The unity we now have and the unity we seek and will also seek with our brothers and

---

See J Runzo, N Martin and A Sharma, editors *Human Rights and Responsibilities in the World Religions* (Oxford: One World, 2003) which is an extended commentary on *A Universal Declaration of Human Rights by the World's Religions* (2000), produced under the leadership of Arvind Sharma.

3. Hans Küng, *A Global Ethic for Global Politics and Economics* (London: SCM, 1997).

4. Peter Singer, *One World: The Ethics of Globalisation* (Melbourne: Text, 2002) grasps this point fully. For a review and critique of Singer see Rowan Gill, *Zadok Perspectives*, 83, Winter 2004, 26–8. One should also attend to John Keane, *Global Civil Society?* (Cambridge: Cambridge University Press, 2003).

sisters of the world is a gift of religious faith: *ad maiorem dei gloriam.*

The aspirations of every single human being can be met from a truly world government, so can the place of groups —and regions, countries and tribes and even trans-national corporations—if their aim is to be part of the family of human beings in their griefs as well as their healing. The world is an aggregate of many diverse peoples with their particular views and aspirations. *E pluribus unum.* From many, one.

The first global statesman was Pope John Paul II (1920–2005). He was multi-lingual—he must have been able to speak about thirty languages—and he touched remarkably every continent of the world with his message of human rights, justice, hope, and peace. His life and witness are a remarkable saga in the life of our modern world. Wojtyla was a complex person and not everyone agreed with him within the Roman Catholic Church, nor would he have an impeccable profile for a papal leader who followed Vatican II. However, all that said, his was a remarkable global leadership. We should not underestimate the influence he brought to bear upon his native Poland and the former Soviet Union in their relinquishment of Communism.[5]

For a week in July 2005 (July 2–9) we saw the possibility and impossibility of world governance and government.

Knowing that the G8, the leaders of the wealthiest nations of the world, would have their annual meeting this year on July 7–9 in Gleneagles, Scotland,[6] the rock music industry of the world lead by Bob Geldof and Bono mounted 'Live 8', a series of massive rock concerts across North America, Europe, South Africa and Japan to influence the G8 leaders (they were not unlike the 'Live Aid' concerts of the 1980s organised by Geldof, for which he was knighted). They were run 'to make poverty

---

5.   Timothy Garton Ash 'John Paul II: The First True Leader of a Fractured World', *The Age,* 5 April 2005, 19; Cardinal Cormac Murphy-O'Connor 'Dynamic Pastor of the Global Village', *The Age,* 4 April 2005, 21; George Weigel, *Witness to Hope: the Biography of John Paul II* (New York: Cliff Street Books, 1999). Timothy Garton Ash is Professor of European Thought at Oxford University. Cormac Murphy-O'Connor is the Cardinal Archbishop of Westminster.

6.   Paul Blustein, 'Will G8 Deliver the Goods?' *The Age,* 11 July 2005, 13.

history', especially in Africa. Bono said, 'We don't want charity, we want justice'.

On Wednesday July 8 the International Olympic Committee meeting in Singapore awarded the 2012 Olympics to London. The people of London—and their representatives in Singapore who had successfully won the bid—were ecstatic. Partying continued all through the night in London.

The next morning, 7/7/2005, Londoners were reduced to fear, shock, trauma and grief when at 9.00 am—the morning peak hour—four young British-born Muslim suicide bombers detonated four bombs in the London transport system, killing indiscriminately upwards of fifty-five people.

British Prime Minister Tony Blair made an impassioned speech to the nation and the world with the leaders of the G8 behind him on the TV screen, George Bush on his right hand, Jacques Chirac on his left. Blair said, 'We will not give in to terror, we will not let terrorists change our values, our civilisation, our way of life'.[7,8]

The final G8 communique from Gleneagles did a number of things. It raised aid to Africa from $US25 billion to $US50 billion by 2010. It gave $US3 billion to the Palestinian Authority to build Gaza after the Israelis leave it. The G8 supported new deals on trade. It cancelled the debt of many of the world's poorest nations (mostly African) and it made possible 100% coverage of AIDS treatment in Africa by 2010. It committed to a peace-keeping force in Africa. It heard African leaders pledge to turn to democracy. The major disappointment was that there was no agreement on climate change, although a conference on it will be held in London on 1 November 2005 for dialogue with the G8 (especially the US) and emerging economies including Brazil, Mexico, China, South Africa and India. Chair of the meeting, Tony Blair, said, 'We speak today in the shadow of terrorism, but it will not obscure what we came here to achieve . . . All of this does not change the world tomorrow—it is a

---

7. Jonathan Freedland, 'The End of an Idyll?' *The Age Insight*, 16 July 2005, 9.
8. Waleed Aly, 'How to Confront a Cult of Terror', *The Age Insight*, 16 July 2005, 9.

beginning, not an end. But it has a pride and a hope and a humanity at its heart that can lift the shadow of terrorism and light the way to a better future.'

Timothy Garton Ash wrote, 'Skilled policing at home, not soldiering abroad, is the way to reduce the threat from the terrorists who operate in our cities'.[9] The West must withdrawn from its colonisation of Palestine, Afghanistan and Iraq.

> Since once again, Lord—though this time not in the forests of Aisne [in France] but in the steppes of Asia—I have neither bread nor wine, nor altar, I will raise myself beyond these symbols, up to the pure majesty of the Real, I, your priest, offer to you on the altar of the entire earth, the travail and suffering of the world. Yonder breaks the sun, to light the uttermost east, and then to send its sheets of fire over the living surface of the earth, which wakens, shudders and resumes its appalling struggle . . . (Pierre Teilhard de Chardin SJ).

---

9.   Timothy Garton Ash, 'The Lesson of London', *The Age*, 12 July 2005, 13.

Conclusion

'In the face of globalisation and the new American empire, we need to counterpose Augustine's counter-empire, the city of God.'[1]

A book on globalisation could not be concluded without a brief discussion of the city of God. 'City of God' is Augustine's term in the treatise of the same name. It is equivalent to the scriptural term 'kingdom of God'. Justice is the gift and task of the city of God.

Any globalising thrust of human reality conjures up the notion of the 'city of God' because the city of God is God's global goal for human life. It is the asymptotic border all seek for but none reach. Many thrust toward it in hubris but as the history of the world shows crumble into ruins.

The empires of men come and go throughout history but the city of God is resplendent over all.

When human reality is examined with the template of the city of God it must be realised that as far as the former is concerned the latter is an eschatological reality. It is the end and goal of human life: it is God's partial gift now and his final gift at the end. The importance of it in the Christian faith is seen by the first words of Jesus in Mark's Gospel: 'The time is fulfilled, and the kingdom of God has come near; repent and believe in the good news'. (Mark 1:15)

Here and now God's representative and foretaste of the city of God on earth is the Christian church. In the city of God Christians are on pilgrimage toward the end, *civitas Dei peregrina*.

---

1. John Milbank, *Being Reconciled: Ontology and Pardon* (London and New York: Routledge, 2003), 210.

Appendix

A number of works have come to hand since I completed this book. Here I address myself to a number of them.

I

William Schweiker, *Theological Ethics and Global Dynamics: In the Time of Many Worlds* (Malden, MA; Oxford; and Carlton, Vic: Blackwell, 2004).

William Schweiker is Professor of Theological Ethics at the University of Chicago. He has written an imposing, very sophisticated and skillful work.

It is obvious that he writes in the shadow of 9/11. He points to a 'twilight' a number of times throughout the book and counsels us to respond to it with joy and, particularly, laughter. He takes Robertson's definition of globalisation: 'a compressed world' or the equivalent of a global village. Our actual world has grown smaller and there are in fact many worlds in which we live and our attention is sought by the peoples in the village. The great problem in this constricted space is 'over-humanisation' which is a great force of human power. This is the picture of globalisation. In this picture of Schweiker's we have the reality about which Schweiker discourses: creation, greed, time, the Golden Rule, love, etc.

Schweiker, in his situation, writes on ethics, a morality; and he imagines a moral cosmology in which people, and not the least, Christians, are to live and be responsible. The underlying reality is 'culture', in which is to be lived the integrity of life. It is a 'political' culture. This is a proving ground of life in which there is to be reconciliation and forgiveness which make for toleration.

The imagination is important. Scripture takes it place within the 'social imaginary' and imagination must be used more extensively in ethics than it was in the past.

Schweiker draws attention to evil as what he calls—in our present situation—'moral madness'. This surd is what we must face with all the force Schweiker allows.

Schweiker is a Christian humanist.

II

Rebecca Todd Peters, *In Search of the Good Life: The Ethics of Globalization* (New York and London: Continuum, 2004).

Todd Peters is Assistant Professor of Religious Studies at Elon University, North Carolina. She puts forward four models of globalisation: the Neo-liberal, the development, the earthist, and the Post-colonial. This book is a treasure trove of information on each paradigm; many resources have been built into this book.

The Neo-liberal view derives from classical economics (as does Development to a certain extent) and she is a strong critic of it for doing virtually nothing to bring democratic power (the solution she advocates in her book) to people. She looks kindly upon those who would develop the lives of peoples but, again, finds their efforts wanting. The earthist position is virtually that of the Greens—working from bottom up instead of top down—and building an economy, at the start, from only two or three people in the face of the hegemon. The Post-colonial position is similar. It is distinctly opposite to colonialism, which is a result of the first two kinds of globalisation.

I did not find a solution in Todd Peters' book, but much to think about.

Here is Todd Peters on the Bible: 'The stories that unfold in the Hebrew Bible and in the New Testament are stories of human accountability and responsibility. While many of these stories open with the mistakes or failings of the characters, Scripture uses these failures as a heuristic device for teaching responsibility' (180).

III

John H Dunning (editor) *Making Globalization Good: The Moral Challenges of Global Capitalism* (Oxford, Oxford University Press, 2004).

This is a fine book by a distinguished group of people, edited by John Dunning who is a Professor of Reading and Rutgers Universities. It is more explicit about the morals of global capitalism than about globalisation.

Dunning means by globalisation the connectivity of institutions and people across the globe, a morally neutral concept (12). He concludes: 'I . . . went on to distinguish between absolute and relative moral values, and argue that globalistion was leading to a convergence of the former, but a divergence of the latter' (32).

Deepak Lal gives a Hindu perspective, and makes an historical critique.

Alan Hamlin gives a closely reasoned account of a conservative economist's position.

Joseph Stiglitz offers us a revision of his October 1998, ninth Rául Prebisch lecture in Geneva. He is most compassionate and finds every conceivable human way to make globalisation work for the benefit of all, as if he were God.

Jack Behrman offers a closely written philosophical account of capitalism and globalisation, making many religious references, without addressing the religions.

Hans Küng repeats his position as stated in the body of my book.

Brian Griffiths, a Christian who is a member of the House of Lords, gives us a layman's Anglican religious view of capitalism.

Khurshid Ahmad makes a very lucid Muslim's account of his religion and the topic. This is one of the clearest and most positive accounts of Islam that I have read.

Jonathan Sacks writes from the Jewish perspective and it is a riveting and gripping account which makes, with Ahmad and Stiglitz, the highlight of the book.

David Loy's is a Buddhist approach and it is productive.

Michael Novak's writing is slick and superficial; he does not sufficiently ground what he calls 'Caritapolis'.

Richard Falk's chapter is about the political relevance of global civil society.

Richard Davies writes as a businessman and therefore discusses the ethics of the business community.

Gordon Brown is the UK Chancellor of the Exchequer. His main solution is for a new 'marshall plan'. He writes very well.

Shirley Williams, the former UK Social Democrats leader who now is in the House of Lords, lifts up a nuanced treatment of social justice.

There are a great many resources in this book besides the text of the articles—long lists of bibliographies after each chapter and extensive notes—and the distinguished company of writers make it an excellent work book. It is 381 pages long.

IV

Peter Heslam (editor) *Globalization and the Good* (Cambridge, UK; Grand Rapids, MI: Eerdmans, 2004).

This is a smaller symposium than the last (11 contributors, 137 pages) but valuable for all that. The book is about 'economic globalisation' (xv-xxi) its pros and cons.

David Held sees the need to be cosmopolitan multilaterally about globalisation and not to approach the matter in the way that the Americans have.

Brian Griffiths writes about trade, aid and domestic reform in the fight against global poverty in which globalisation has resulted for many. Africa must come, some time, to 'owning its own development' (25).

Clive Mather gives us a business response to globalisation; principle and profit can be combined.

Michael Woolcock says we must go beyond justice to glory: 'So glory in what we might call the Grandeur Tradition of Scripture is about God's otherness, omnipotence and omnipresence. If the Grandeur Tradition is not something we can fully comprehend, then perhaps that is exactly as it should be: God is God, and we are not' (43). This Tradition is the grace tradition. Woolcock's contribution is very thought-provoking; especially about the preferential option for the poor.

Ann Pettifor writes about the great transformation – putting human rights before money rights. She introduces Moltmann's notion of the Sabbath as a renewing of all creation.

Michael Schluter offers a Biblical critique of global capital markets.

Theologian Timothy Gorringe addresses the topic of the 'principalities and powers'.

Cynthia Moe-Lobeda brings to bear immanentist Luther themes on the topic. 'God is boundless, justice-seeking love coursing through creation implies that all creatures and elements may offer creative, saving, sustaining power towards creation's flourishing' (100).

Michael Taylor offers practical advice about campaigning against injustice and appealing to self interest.

Jim Wallis, the progressive American Evangelical whose important books are *The Soul of Politics* (1994) and *God's Politics* (2005) writes on the role of prophetic witness and faith-based initiatives in tackling inequality. His chapter is a delight to read.

To complete the book Peter Heslam sounds the note of sustainability.

V

Eugene McCarraher, 'The Enchantments of Mammon: Notes Toward a Theological History of Capitalism', *Modern Theology* Vol 21, No 3 (July 2005), 429–461.

This article is about the religious assumptions and trappings about all the discussions and actions of capitalism over the past 150 years, including Marx. After this essay readers will want to read: Stephen Pattison, *The Faith of the Managers: When Management Becomes Religion* (London and Washington: Cassell, 1997).

VI

Guen-Seok Yang, 'Globaliszation and Christian Responses: Korea', *Theology Today* 62 (April 2005), 38-48.

This is a practical essay about the Protestant Church in South Korea. Through globalisation a mono-cultural society has changed to a multicultural one very rapidly in which the church must offer mission/service to those who have come from North Korea and other Asian countries to make up a substantial part of the workforce.

VII

Mary C Grey, *Sacred Longings: Ecofeminist Theology and Globalization* (London: SCM Press, 2003).

This book is a fine and challenging work. Globalisation is assumed to be the enemy, particularly in Europe and India where Grey has the most practical experience. More than ethics are needed (194), rather a full blown spirituality which Grey develops. She does this through scripture, myth, story and poetry. In the end she has developed a strong bulwark against the enemy. She is an eco feminist so she takes seriously the woman's point of view and liberation from patriarchy, and caring for the earth in every possible way. It is her eco feminism which is the strong force resulting in the powerful spirituality in and of this book.

Grey is a theologian, but one not frightened to get her hands dirty in the process of theologising. She has held many distinguished positions in the UK and Holland and is currently Professor of Pastoral Theology at the University of Wales, Lampeter. Grey and her husband are both trustees of an NGO 'Wells for India' sited in Rajasthan in North West India.

She says 'we are a broken-hearted culture' (x). Her intent is to heal a maimed world and she goes about it spiritually to spirituality. Throughout the book the theme of the dearth of water runs, through the land she writes about and through her thinking which has the impulse of and leads to a spirituality of water through the Holy Spirit.

The book is comprehensive and encapsulates the situation in the world and the solution to the world's situation in love, joy and peace—in God—very well.

Finally she traverses well people's longing—longing for goodness, spirit, redemption—and God through Christ.

VIII

There is an historical background to the globalisation of the twentieth and twenty-first centuries which Jürgen Osterhammel and Niels Petersson both of the University of Konstanz have sketched.[1] They say that globalisation has existed for seven or eight centuries. We will let them speak for themselves:

> We distinguish between four major periods. Until the mid-eighteenth century, empire-building, trade, and religious solidarity encouraged inter-

---

1.   Jürgen Osterhammel and Niels P Petersson, *Globalization: a Short History*, translated by Dona Geyer (Princeton and Oxford: Princeton University Press, 2005).

continental exchange on an expanding scale. From about the 1750s onward, political revolution in the Americas and in Europe intensified imperial rivalry, and the Industrialization of some parts of the Northern Hemisphere created networks of traffic, communication, migration, and commerce that in density and strength surpassed anything known up to that time. Our third period begins in the 1880s and lasts until the end of World War II. Its main features were the politicization of globalization through attempts to turn it into an instrument of national policies; the seemingly final division of the world among the imperialist great powers; and the growth of global flows of capital and the rise of programs envisaging the re-ordering of the entire globe in terms of liberalism (Woodrow Wilson) or revolutionary socialism (Lenin). The 1930s and early 1940s witnessed a catastrophic breakdown of global-ization. Characteristically, however, the crisis and conflicts of those years were of a truly worldwide scope. The fourth period, beginning in 1945, was dominated by attempts to avoid mistakes made during the period between the two world wars. While the world economy was reconstructed along liberal lines, the antagonism of the American-led "free world" and the Soviet bloc during the Cold War prevented many potential relations and linkages from unfolding. This is why we speak of "globalization split in two". During this fourth period, mass tourism, the rise of global media and global forms of entertainment, and the spread of Western patterns of consumption were already pointing toward the kind of everyday experience characteristic of the early twenty-first century. Problems such as environmental damage, competition over scarce resources (oil, for example), and even terrorism began to assume a trans-continental

character. By the early 1980s many of the
elements of contemporary globalization were in
place (ix–xi).

Obviously the authors have not brought their history right
up to the present in the Preface, although there is an excellent
discussion of the concept of globalisation in chapter 1, a good
and helpful outline of historiography—how to sketch the
history of globalization—in chapter 2, and a challenging
outlook on the present in the last chapter (chapter 7, the
conclusion):

It is difficult to find any empirical evidence to support the
more extravagant analyses of present-day globalization offered
by some theorists. In many cases, these analyses are more
accurately described as predictions or depictions of utopias,
positive as well as negative ones (chapter 7, 147).

The final paragraph of the book is most thought-provoking:
globalisation is just like everything else, it will go down in
history like industrialisation and urbanisation, etc.

Rowan Gill
September 2005.